BARBECUE
with an International flavour

BARBECUE
with an International flavour

by Maggie Black

W. Foulsham & Co. Ltd.

London · New York · Toronto · Cape Town · Sydney

This book is for Robert and Alex in England and James and Emma in Australia

W. FOULSHAM & COMPANY LIMITED
Yeovil Road, Slough, Berkshire, SL1 4JH

ISBN 0-572-01215-2

Photoset in Great Britain by Rowland Phototypesetting Limited, Bury St Edmunds, Suffolk
and printed in Hong Kong by Colorcraft Ltd.

ACKNOWLEDGEMENTS

The patient testing, tasting and typing of several good friends have helped to create this book. I should like to thank in particular Joanne Jones in Texas, and my South African, Greek and Australian friends and family; also Pauline Wilson for both testing recipes and typing the manuscript.

I owe a special debt to Frank Odell who has personally given me much good advice as well as photographs and gear from his company for testing and photography; to Jim Marks of Weber Distribution Ltd, whose barbecuing technique and equipment I have admired for years; and to many colleagues who provided products or photographs and patiently answered my questions about recipes they supplied. I should mention: Stork Cookery Service (pages 34, 35); Van den Bergh's Ltd. (pages 33, 76); British Chicken (pages 60, 64, cover, bottom left); British Turkey Federation (pages 57, 61); New Zealand Lamb Information Bureau (pages 39, 49, 56); Butter Information Council (pages 37, 73); Gale's Honey Bureau (pages 40, 41, 62); British Bacon Bureau (page 42); British Sausage Bureau (pages 44, 54, cover, bottom right); Canned Food Advisory Service (page 69); Mazola Ltd. (pages 48, 59); Jif Lemon Juice (page 69); Danish Agricultural Producers (pages 70, 75); Hellman's Mayonnaise (page 71); Dutch Dairy Bureau (page 74); Thermos Ltd.; McCormicks Spices; Colman's of Norwich (cover, top left); Mushroom Growers' Association (page 33); Frank Odell Ltd. (pages 53, 63); Rex Bamber (pages 36, 46, 51, cover, top right).

Finally my thanks to Brooks Productions Ltd, for persuading me to try barbecuing in England, and for all the pleasure I've had from it.

Maggie Black

CONTENTS

WHY BARBECUE?

Barbecuing is popular the world over simply because it handles top-quality foods in the best possible way. Sealing in all their natural juices and goodness, it cooks them just to the point each person prefers, plain or spiced as he wishes. Every people in the world barbecues food in some fashion for this reason, using the favourite local spices and seasonings. Each adds its special personal signature to the craft of barbecue cooking as I hope the recipes I have chosen show.

Barbecuing is popular too because it's informal. Kindling a fire gives one a sense of adventure, of triumphant excitement when the fuel 'catches'. The glowing coals, rising smoke, and aroma of cooking in outdoor air are natural elements. One can't be formal while grilling a chop on a brazier or stand on ceremony when eating it in one's fingers. Barbecuing is fun and relaxing.

Barbecuing handles cheaper foods just as effectively as prime cuts. Peoples in hot countries where all food is precious and must be used soon know it well. They have made an art of kebab cooking for miscellaneous 'bits'. You'll find examples from South Africa, Indonesia, and the Middle East among others in this book.

Even using top-grade meat, barbecuing is a cheap way of entertaining. A barbecue itself is not expensive; you can even build your own, and the equipment can be just your ordinary kitchen gear. Cardboard plates, mugs and paper napkins are quite adequate – and fingers are the best forks for barbecued food.

What's more you save money (and calories if you're slimming) because barbecued foods need so few extras. A salad, fresh fruit, bread and butter are quite enough, and simple drinks such as beer or cider and coffee. If you want to serve an elaborate 'starter' or dessert you can, but there's no need.

Barbecuing does more than produce superb food simply and cheaply. It's a real release for the home cook, chorewise. There is no table to lay, the equipment is easy to set up, and there's almost no washing-up. All the food can be prepared ahead and stacked in the refrigerator, or can come from the freezer ready to use. The cook has no last-minute cooking to do. In fact she may not have to cook at all, because a husband, friends or children are usually willing to take over the grilling. Most men thoroughly enjoy barbecuing.

One pleasant aspect of a barbecue party is that you needn't worry if one or two extra turn up, or about latecomers. It's also an ideal way to entertain semi-strangers or foreigners. Anyone from almost anywhere understands how to barbecue, and feels at home doing it.

Barbecuing cuts out other problems besides coping with strangers. Once you've got it organised, you can smile at power cuts. You can even laugh at the weather. Don't think that you can only barbecue on tropic-hot summer evenings. Most barbecues fit onto quite a small verandah, and can operate there even if the Heavens open! And why not make a winter bonfire party a barbecue when everyone's muffled up in duffles and boots anyway? Or you could bring the outdoors indoors with a gas-fired barbecue in the fireplace.

One way or another, barbecuing offers you cheerful, relaxed good eating anytime, anywhere – as people around the globe have known for centuries.

CHOOSING A BARBECUE

When you first look at barbecues, your choice seems immensely wide. Each model seems to have different design details which may be useful in the kind of barbecuing you want to do.

The first thing to be sure about is that you really do want to barbecue. For this reason, and because of cost, most people start by trying out the simplest kind of portable barbecue or even make an impromptu one. Then very little is lost if you find that barbecuing doesn't give you the value you hoped for; on the other hand, if you decide to go on to buying a more elaborate barbecue nothing is lost either, because your first barbecue can be used for keeping food warm, or can be pressed into service when you have more people to feed than the new model can cope with. It can, being compact and portable, be used for picnics or indoors.

In several ways, it is better to have two smaller models than one big one. Groups of barbecuers split up instead of huddling round one barbecue, and there is a lot more standing space around the two barbecues for them to do their own grilling. By having two fires, the very hot central fire area for open grilling (page 20) is available to more people and the cooler edges of the fire used for foil and skewer cooking is almost doubled in area.

Before you set about having any barbecue, consider the following points:

Can it be moved?
A portable barbecue can be taken on picnics, to the beach etc, if not too large or ungainly; bricks or blocks used to build an impromptu barbecue may be too heavy to shift. A barbecue on wheels can be trundled about and moved if the wind changes but should have a foldaway undercarriage for transport by car or for storage. A waggon barbecue is heavy and can only be pushed over level ground.

Is it strong and stable?
Heavy gauge metal or cast iron does not warp with heat, although heavy to carry. Sturdy chrome-plated grills with close-set rods are much better than lightweight ones. Any

Brazier barbecue

wheel-base or stand must both be sturdy and stable; dangerous accidents can occur if a barbecue topples over.

Is it convenient to cook on?
Unless you have a stone slab or metal-topped table to stand a table model on, cooking must be done squatting or crouching over the barbecue. However, a table model is easier to fit into a fireplace indoors and is also easier to protect from draughts.

Is the fire easy to manage?
Dampers are desirable for ventilating the fire, both to get it going and to control the degree of heat. One should also be able to raise or lower the grill for more or less cooking heat as needed. A wind-shield or hood is a plus because both the top and the sides of the fire and food are protected from wind-gusts more efficiently than by a firebreak.

Is it the right shape?
You will get more food items on a circular grill than on a square or rectangular one of the same area. People can gather round a circular barbecue more easily too. However a rectangular barbecue may fit your scene better. It is neater since it can be tucked against a wall, and it usually fits into a fireplace more easily. It is also neater and easier to store.

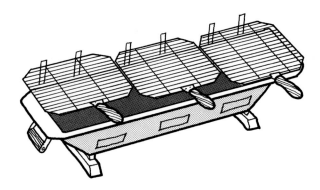

Hibachi barbecue

TYPES YOU CAN BUY
Hibachis
These are the simplest and cheapest barbecue to buy, and therefore the best known. The hibachi came from Japan, and its name means 'fire-box' in Japanese. It is basically just what it says, namely a fire-box, which should be at least 3 in/7.5 cm deep, with one, two or three grills on top depending on its shape and size. Round hibachis are generally quite small and only cook food for 4–6 people, but rectangular ones with 'double' or 'triple' grills and pans are now popular since one grill can be lifted off to remove cooked food without disturbing the others. A small fire just for family cooking can be made under one of the grills only so the larger sizes of hibachi are no more extravagant on fuel.

A hibachi is generally made from heavy cast iron although lighter pressed steel and aluminium models can now be bought. Some models have a foldaway stand or detachable legs on wheels. All have draught controls which help to get the fire lighted and to control its rate of burning.

Table or picnic barbecues
These are small lightweight barbecues designed for packing in the car boot or in one's rucksack. There are various designs but most have a shallow tray rather than a fire-box, and a 12 in/30 cm grill which will cook food for about 4 people. Some grills revolve so that you need not lean over the fire to get at food items.

Brazier or 'party' barbecues
The simplest brazier barbecues are very like picnic barbecues but are on removable legs or a stand. Better models have wheels. The height of the grill can be altered on most models. Some have a wind-shield with holes for a spit, and some have a useful small work-surface or shelf for holding tools or a jug of 'baste'. A large party brazier may be 24 in/60 cm in diameter and can cook food for up to 20 people. There are a great many different designs.

Hooded barbecues
These may have a whole or a half-hood like a covered windshield. One advantage of a half-hood is that it pro-

Half-hooded barbecue

A simple waggon barbecue

Square kettle barbecue

tects the fire and food from cold gusts of wind, saves smoke swirling in the barbecuers' faces and provides support and mountings for a battery-operated spit – yet you can still see the food cooking and baste it as you wish. Barbecues with a hood may also have an 'oven' space in the top part for keeping plates and cooked food warm, which means that cooking can be done in stages instead of when people are clamouring to eat. Most models have folding legs with wheels, the hood is often detachable and a useful work-shelf is included at the side or underneath.

Most hooded barbecues are fairly large with a 22–24 in/55–50 cm grill, and cook a simple meal for 16–20 people.

Kettle barbecues

These are both the most efficient hooded barbecues and the best looking. They are most often globe-shaped, and the best models are generally made of weather-proof porcelain-enamelled steel, in attractive vivid colours. They have detachable legs with wheels. The domed top half lifts off, exposing the grill ready for ordinary use over a deep fire-bowl. With the lid on, reflected heat from it effectively tenderises and browns the meat like an oven, making it possible to cook large joints from scratch with a true barbecued flavour. You avoid pre-cooking in the oven and the risk of letting them cool.

Both the deep fire-bowl and the lid of a kettle have adjustable vents to control the air-flow. This means that the cook can raise or lower the heat as he or she wishes and quench the flames entirely when cooking is done, thus saving any unused fuel.

The round kettle barbecues are usually 18–22 in/45–55 cm in diameter and cook a meal for 16–20 people.

Waggon barbecues

These are large covered barbecues mounted on a wheeled trolley, usually rectangular. They are luxurious, fitted with features such as see-through glass doors, built-in storage cabinets, a warming oven, work shelf and temperature gauge. More important the distance between the grill and fire is adjustable and, like the kettle barbecue, heat control is efficient even in bad weather. However, a waggon barbecue is weighty, and although it has wheels is not suitable for dragging over rough ground, so its use is really confined to a verandah or perhaps by a swimming pool. Storage may be a problem too, unless you have a spare garage or stable space.

Gas-fired barbecues

These, again, are luxury products. Most look like braziers or hooded barbecues, but they do not use charcoal. The heat is provided by lava or artificial rock which does not burn but is heated almost instantly by a gas burner. As on an oven, the temperature is controlled simply by turning a knob which gives you a choice of high or low heat. These barbecues have another advantage in that they do not give off noxious fumes like charcoal so they are safe to use anywhere – as well as at a moment's notice. The bottled gas is in a clip-on cylinder underneath.

The main disadvantages of a gas-fired barbecue, like a waggon barbecue, are its cost and the fact that it is rather like bringing a compact modern kitchen outdoors. One admires the slick performance but the 'feel' of outdoor cooking as a spontaneous adventure is lost.

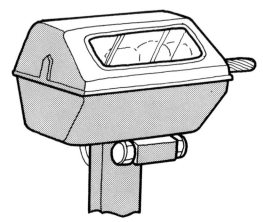

Gas-fired barbecue with a see-through door. The cylinder of calor gas is attached below.

BUILDING A BARBECUE

IMPROMPTU BARBECUES

A barbecue is only a container for burning charcoal with a grid on top, so it is easy to build an impromptu one if you want to find out whether open-air charcoal cookery will be your 'scene' or not.

Give it a fair trial though. It is often said that you can make a barbecue out of an old biscuit tin or flower pot. But neither really gives you enough grilling area to cook more than two small items at a time, so your meal will be laborious to make. A large solid roasting tin or the urn type of concrete garden plant-holder is a better bet, or just a frame of loose bricks with a few air-holes between them. In Africa the bottom of a 4-gallon petrol drum is sometimes used.

If you use a tin or drum, punch holes in the bottom and sides, and raise the tin off the ground on a few bricks or flat-topped stones, to let air in. Then lay a large cake cooling rack or metal refrigerator shelf on top to hold the food. Doubled chicken wire held taut by wire will do, or mesh burglar-proofing.

Another sensible idea is to use an old metal wheelbarrow. Make the bottom level with large flat stones, or prop up the wheel end. Light the fire inside, and put a grill rack on top extending over the barrow's sides. One bonus of this barbecue is that you can wheel the used fuel right to the rubbish tip.

Use charcoal briquettes or lumps (page 18) as fuel for your equipment. It's an appealing idea to build an impromptu barbecue on the beach, or by the river if you've had a decent catch. There's no problem about the container. A ring of stones with one or two spaces between them will serve. Dry fuel, however, may be impossible to find. Really dry driftwood doesn't lie about in heaps on the seashore, and except in a drought, a quantity of twigs and branches dry enough to burn may take hours of searching for. Don't risk spoiling your first enthusiasm by making a fire which just won't light or which, if it does, spoils your food by smothering it (and you) in smoke.

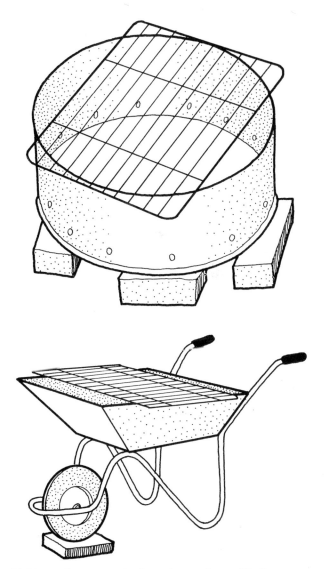

Making an impromptu barbecue is a good way of finding out whether you enjoy barbecuing.

A PERMANENT BARBECUE

If you really get smitten with barbecuing, you may decide to build a permanent barbecue at home. It can make good sense because it will add an attractive selling feature to your property as well as a pleasant feature of garden design, and when you're not using it for cooking, it will be a tidy place to burn garden rubbish.

If you have a large verandah, you could build one like a fireplace into one end wall of it; but barbecues of this type are usually gas-fired, have an extractor fan to get rid of fumes and are expensive. A charcoal-fired garden barbecue is easier and cheaper to build and just as much fun to use.

You must make quite sure before you start that you pick a suitable place for it because you can't tear it down and start again.

The spot you choose should be out of the prevailing wind, but not wholly protected from breezes because you'll need a draught for fire-lighting and blowing away smoke. Preferably it should be fairly near the kitchen door to make fetching and carrying easy – say on the edge of a pathway running from the back door along the side of the house. It is better built against a wall than free-standing.

Probably the best way to find the best spot in your garden is to set up an impromptu barbecue in various likely places and see which scores highest for general convenience.

You might think that having selected your site the next thing to do is to design the barbecue. Not so! Get your grill first – better still, 2 or 3 grills – because they will dictate the size of your barbecue. If you want one, get a spit too because its length will determine the width of your barbecue. You must be able to fit it onto supports attached to the side walls. Visit a local scrap metal yard or builder's yard, and see if you can lay hands on a derelict cooker or refrigerator. Chrome-plated refrigerator shelves make excellent grills, and an oven lining can supply a base for your fire area. An old roasting tin does as a fire-pan.

If possible, get building materials which tone in with your house and garden architecture for building your barbecue, and try to afford fire bricks to line the fire area. If these are too expensive, see if you can get broken fire bricks or tiles or oven-burnt bricks from a brickyard.

Your fire area should be like a large open box, only very slightly bigger than your grills all round. Before you build it, see that, if possible, there is enough space to build a fuel and firelighter store alongside it. This will be the easiest way to have a dry, warm fuel supply always to hand, and to keep any inflammable liquids outside the house; also if you roof it with a paving slab or concrete garden table top it will make a valuable working shelf beside the barbecue. It should have a hinged weatherproof door to keep the fuel dry.

Build this cupboard first so that one side of it 'doubles' as one side of your fire area. The other side should be a double-thickness brick wall built to match. As you build these side walls, fit in flanges on which two grills can rest at different levels (make sure they are at equal heights so that the grills are not tilted). Also build in two wide-angle brackets at the top of the barbecue which, with notches in the top, will hold your spit. Bury the short arm of each bracket in the concrete below the top course of bricks so that the arms project just above the barbecue. Complete your barbecue with a triple course of bricks across the front at the bottom.

If you have built on grass, your building materials will probably wreck it. Don't try to nurse it back to health. It will only get worn bare, greasy, slippery and charred by your barbecuing activities. Be bold and pave the area instead; it is easier to wash down than gravel.

Plan and build your barbecue carefully as you will not be able to alter it once it is finished.

13

GETTING READY TO BARBECUE – EQUIPMENT

So you've decided to barbecue! Whatever barbecue you have chosen, the gear you'll need is much the same. Whether you've decided to give a full-scale party or simply to give the family a barbecued Sunday lunch, the basic equipment you'll need is much the same too. Only the scale of your operations will vary.

You'll need four kinds of equipment for any barbecuing: equipment for handling the fire and barbecue; cooking equipment; serving equipment; diners' equipment. These are listed below with a few notes on each and drawings to identify them. Use these lists as check lists before you start cooking to make sure you've assembled everything you need.

Kitchen supply shops will offer many more barbecuing accessories than are given here. When you become a confirmed barbecuing addict, you may want to buy some of them. But you can barbecue equally well with just your standard kitchen tools provided they are sturdy and you don't mind them getting tough wear. If you intend to do a lot of barbecuing, you may be well advised to get hard-wearing chef's kitchen tools and keep them in a special box so that they're always ready for use.

Most of the equipment is shown in the photographs accompanying the recipes.

EQUIPMENT FOR HANDLING THE FIRE AND BARBECUE
Tongs, poker
You will need tongs for spreading the coals and for moving single lumps of charcoal. Use a poker for flicking grey ash off the fire, but not for spreading it.
Bellows
Draughts or just the passing of time may cool your fire before cooking is finished. Blowing on it is hot and dirty work.

Shovel
You will need a small shovel both for putting more coals on the fire and for removing hot ash afterwards.
Aluminium foil
Lining the barbecue with foil will make cleaning up much easier. It's essential for making foil food parcels too.
Protective gloves, cloths
NEVER attempt to touch any part of a barbecue or hot pans, forks or skewers with bare hands. Remember that a barbecue stays very hot for ages.
Sprinkler bottle for water
You must be able to douse any small flare-ups which occur. Use a bottle with a spray or sprinkler top such as an old insecticide sprayer.
Pile of sand or old barbecue cinders
You will need this for dousing the fire after use. This is better than water, which may damage the barbecue.
Cleaning materials
Your normal cleaning materials, a wire brush, detergent, oven cleaner. See *Clearing Up*, page 78.

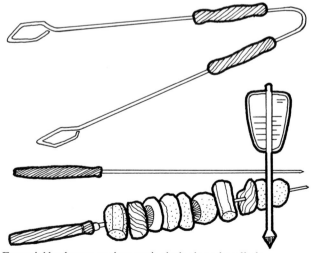

Essential barbecue equipment includes long-handled tongs, various types of skewers and, for spit-roasting, a meat thermometer.

COOKING EQUIPMENT

Spit and motor (battery or electric)
This is, of course, optional, but most barbecues except the simplest hibachis have a place where a spit can be inserted. Many come equipped with a spit but not a motor. Luxury barbecues may have an electric spit motor but it ties you to barbecuing within reach of a power supply.

Drip tray
A drip tray is essential for spit-roasting, but not otherwise necessary.

Meat thermometer
Not essential but helpful if spit-roasting.

Toasting tongs, spatula
You'll need several pairs of tongs. Never turn meat over by piercing it with a fork; always use tongs, or a broad slice or spatula.

Kebab and other long skewers
You'll need plenty for all kebab cooking. Meatballs are best cooked on special flattened skewers broader at one end than the other. For solid meat kebabs, very long ordinary round skewers are cheap and easy to buy.

Double-sided grill
A double-sided hinged grill which holds the food between two layers of mesh is almost essential if you want to barbecue soft or thin items like burgers or fish which may break up.

Long-handled fork, carving knife, board
You'll need a carving knife and fork for carving meat on the spit, and a large board for slicing meats grilled or spit-roasted in one large piece.

Aluminium foil
See above. Also have paper towels and rags available for mopping up drips etc.

Sharp knives
Although it's wise to cut steaks and kebab meats to grilling size ahead of time (page 28), you should have sharp knives available for doing last-minute trimming, cutting up large cooked portions etc.

Basting brush or mop, jug
You'll need one for each special 'baste' you use and one for

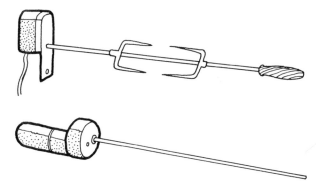

Most barbecues have a place for a spit, and some more sophisticated models also have an electric spit motor.

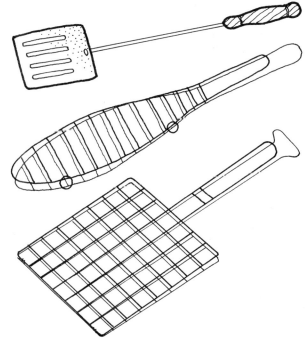

A double-sided hinged grill is ideal for soft or thin items which may otherwise break up while cooking.

15

plain melted butter or oil. A washing-up brush or mop is a better way to apply a 'baste' than a tube baster because it has a handle.

Gloves, aprons
If just one or two people are doing the cooking, they'll need gloves when handling the grill, hot skewers, etc, and aprons to protect their clothes from drips of fat and basting sauce.

Cooks' table, containers or trays, saucepans
Put the raw food for barbecuing on a trestle table or trolley with a plastic cloth on it. Lay the food in easy-clean containers or on trays. Have bastes, melted butter etc in heavy saucepans which will stand level on the grill (don't use ones with plastic handles).

Protective food coverings
Use decorators' plastic sheets to cover tables etc set up ahead of time. Keep raw food protected from pets and pests until cooking time by laying foil over it with shelves from your oven or cake cooling trays on top.

Spices and seasonings
Besides salt and pepper, offer cooks a choice of dried herbs and spices which will suit the food being barbecued. Some big firms offer a suitable selection in a neat rack.

SERVING EQUIPMENT
Serving table
Put salads, breads and other ready-to-use foods on a separate table from raw foods, especially if you have a crowd.

Salad bowls, fruit bowls, bread basket, cake cover
Use sturdy containers, avoiding glass or plastic. Put bread or rolls in a basket, not on a plate or board. Keep desserts covered with a plastic cake cover.

Insulated pitchers, jugs
Keep hot foods such as soups or sauces hot in insulated pitchers. Pour a little into a jug as needed.

Bar table, ice bucket, can and bottle openers
Keep drinks away from the food to disperse numbers.

Coffee or tea pot, milk, sugar
Keep coffee or tea hot in insulated containers.

Freezer bag, cold packs
Butter, cream or salads will keep fresher and free from flies in a freezer bag with a frozen cold pack in it.

Serving tools for salads, gâteaux etc.
Use sturdy cheap plastic ones in bright colours to prevent their getting lost.

Kitchen paper, tea towels
Useful for spills.

Condiments, relishes
Use a big kitchen salt cellar and pepper mill which are easy to spot on the table. Put relishes in sturdy jam jars, clearly labelled.

DINERS' EQUIPMENT
Cardboard plates, mugs
Disposable plates and mugs are a better idea than plastic ones which may get crushed underfoot.

Paper napkins
Supply plenty of sturdy ones.

Cutlery
Most barbecue fare is finger-food but sharp knives and forks will be needed for steaks, extra forks for a salad or gâteau, spoons for coffee. Get more than you think you'll need. They tend to get left about.

Aluminium foil, kitchen paper roll
Have several rolls of foil around, for wrapping drumstick ends, etc. Kitchen paper can be used for spills.

Waste bags or bin
If chop bones, used napkins, plates, etc are tipped straight into a waste bag or bin, they can be disposed of easily.

Mosquito/fly sprays
Spray the air around the serving table occasionally (*not* the food).

SAFETY

Barbecuing is perfectly safe provided you guard against a few obvious fire risks. It is a good idea to make a list of simple safety rules and make sure that children, especially, read and understand them before barbecuing.

SET UP THE BARBECUE IN A SAFE PLACE

1. Site a portable barbecue in the open air, on a patio with one side open to the air, or in a room with all the windows open. Burning charcoal gives off carbon monoxide which can be dangerous.
2. See that the barbecue is clear of overhanging trees or low dry bushes, and that the area is free of dry leaves, grass or twigs which could catch fire. Clear up periodically any disposable plates, paper napkins or rags lying around near the barbecue.
3. Do not site the barbecue on slippery or cobbled ground, or on any kind of wooden or vinyl-covered flooring. A level paved or concrete floor is best; make sure the barbecue stands level and is stable on its legs.
4. A strong draught or breeze can rekindle charcoal, and may blow smoke and sparks into people's faces. Put up an adequate flameproof wind-break, if necessary.
5. Never move a lighted barbecue if you can help it; if you must shift it make sure the wind is at your back.

LIGHT THE FIRE CAREFULLY

Never use petrol, kerosene, lighter fluid, naptha or any volatile fuel to get the fire started. They are not only dangerous, they make the food taste unpleasant. (See page 18.)

WATCH OUT – IT'S HOT!

1. Wear heavy oven-gloves to touch any part of a barbecue after the fire has been lit, and even after it seems to have died down. In daylight, it is impossible to 'see' red-hot charcoal; it will appear white and powdery even if giving off extreme heat. The grill and fire-pan can be almost red-hot too without looking it.

2. Don't equip the barbecue with metal or plastic-handled tools, pans or spoons which hold the heat or melt. Use long-handled tongs and other tools if possible.
3. Douse any small flare-ups from dripping fat with a sprinkling of water as soon as they occur, and use a drip tray for spit-roasting. A small pile of sand or old barbecue cinders will smother burning fat.
4. Prevention is better than cure but keep a tube of burn salve handy in case of stinging small burns from sparks or from touching the barbecue accidentally.

Barbecuing is perfectly safe as long as you remember the simple safety precautions. Never forget that that barbecue itself gets very hot so you need gloves and long-handled tools.

FUEL AND FIRE

Most people use charcoal for barbecuing because it is fairly cheap and is easy to use and store, but you can use wood if you want to, say for a spontaneous, spur-of-the moment barbecue.

WOOD

Softwoods such as cedar or birch can be used to get a wood fire going because they burn fast, but the resin they contain makes them smoke heavily, give off sparks and flare easily, so they are not suitable for the main fire. Pine or eucalyptus should never be used, as Australians know well, because they make the food taste of cough-mixture.

Hardwoods such as oak, ash and beech which contain little resin burn more slowly and give a hotter fire; a few sprigs of an aromatic herb such as bay or rosemary added to the fire scent the surrounding air and the food even more romantically than the 'bonfire' smell of the hard-woods. However, if you want a scented (wood *or* charcoal) fire it is usually more practical to buy packeted woods and herbs specially chosen and dried for sprinkling on a fire (page 29).

Any wood used for a barbecue or camp-fire must be dry, solid not crumbling, and clean: rotten wood smells awful. A local timber-yard may supply shavings, chips and small off-cuts. Otherwise, use twigs, leaves and bark to start the fire, then add larger twigs and well-dried branches. Pile up a good supply of fuel before you even attempt to start your fire. You will need more than you think.

CHARCOAL

There are two kinds of charcoal: lump charcoal made from both softwoods and hardwoods, and charcoal briquettes made from hardwoods such as beech or oak which are sold in uniform blocks or nuggets. Lump charcoal lights easily and burns fast so is good for getting a fire going, but it may include lumps made from softwoods which smoke, flare and give off sparks. It burns about twice as fast as briquettes so you need twice as much of it.

Briquettes consist of compressed charcoal and may contain some coal waste. They are easier than lumps to arrange in a compact 'bed', being all the same size, and they burn slowly and evenly, giving off an intense heat without smoke or flames – which is what you want for barbecuing. They need less attention, too, than lump charcoal.

It is cheaper to buy briquettes in bulk than in small bags, but you must have a dry storage place for them. Even slightly damp charcoal will create clouds of smoke without really getting set well alight.

FIRELIGHTERS

Lighting a charcoal barbecue fire is child's play using modern firelighters. There is no need to use dangerous 'starters' such as methylated spirit or lighter fuel or, worse, to soak charcoal in a bucket of petrol. Unless you possess a portable electric fire-starter or gas blow-lamp, and know how to use it, use either self-igniting charcoal briquettes or the commonplace solid block white firelighters, also available as granules. Jellied alcohol is another choice.

Gas-fired barbecues (page 10) which are simply lighted by turning a knob are of course foolproof (unless you run out of bottled gas).

BUILDING THE FIRE

Charcoal needs bottom ventilation to get started. If your barbecue has one or more damper, open them. Cover a solid fire-pan with foil which reflects heat upward, then with gravel which provides a little upward draught and mops up grease spills (you can wash and re-use it). A pair of bellows provides a manpower draught.

Place on this 'bed' either a few balls of crushed newspaper and wood chips (for wood fires); or a few bits (not many) of broken-up solid block firelighter or a handful of granules and some charcoal fragments (for charcoal fires). Cover with a small pile of charcoal (beginners usually use too much). Light the fire with a taper.

When you light your fire will depend on its size, the type of barbecue and fuel and the weather. Lump charcoal takes longer to get going than briquettes and any charcoal burns more slowly on a cold or damp day. A barbecue fire for grilling should be ready to cook on in 35 to 40 minutes using lump charcoal and in 25 to 35 minutes using briquettes, provided the fuel is dry. A fire for spit-roasting will take longer. Most manufacturers of larger covered, kettle or waggon barbecues tell you in their instruction leaflets how long to allow for the fire to reach cooking heat. A gas-fired barbecue gives you adequate cooking heat in just 5 minutes on average.

As soon as the fire has caught, spread the charcoal out into an even layer with long-handled tongs. Leave a bit of space at the sides of the fire-pan for more fuel. Always add fuel at the sides, never on top of the fire, because that smothers the heat. Keep a supply of lumps or briquettes warm right beside the barbecue, and add a few to the fire if the coal level burns low.

If you will be cooking for some hours or spit-roasting, you will need more fuel than for a quick barbecued family supper. For spit-roasting, spread the fire across the back of the barbecue parallel with the spit and put a drip-tray under the spit itself to catch drops of grease.

Note that in daylight the charcoal will not appear to be burning at all. You can only tell it is burning if it has what seems to be a film of white ash on top of the charcoal.

To judge whether the fire is hot enough to cook on, see the cooking instructions on page 20. If you think it is not hot enough and want to cook quickly, open dampers, flick off any white ash with a poker or give the fire a puff or two of air with bellows. To cool it a little, raise the grill an inch or two, or if it is fixed, move the food to the side of the fire where it is cooler.

DOUSING THE FIRE

Put out the fire as soon as cooking is finished because you can then use the coals again. Don't use water for dousing. It may damage a hot metal or brick barbecue, and the wet fuel will take a long time to dry. Shovel the burning fuel into a bucket or a metal wheelbarrow, then smother it with old barbecue cinders. This method lets you clean up the barbecue itself quickly (page 78) and you can use the ashes from the fire on the garden.

Build the fire gradually, and do not use too much charcoal at the beginning.

COOKING ON YOUR BARBECUE

There are four main ways of cooking on your barbecue: open grilling; cooking in foil; kebab or skewer cooking; and spit-roasting.

Open grilling is best suited to firm, flat pieces of meat such as steaks, chops or sausages. Large joints can be partly pre-cooked in the oven, then finished off on the barbecue.

Foil-cooking is used for thin or soft pieces of food which may break up or dry out in cooking such as fish fillets or thin strips of liver.

Kebab cookery is used for bite-sized bits of solid meat or vegetables, or for minced meat.

Spit-roasting by contrast is used for large pieces such as a whole chicken or joint.

FOOD TEMPERATURE

Thaw any frozen meat or fish you will barbecue thoroughly, and bring it to room temperature before cooking. The only exception is thin items such as gammon rashers or chicken breasts. If you want them crusty-brown outside but still juicy within, cook them straight from the refrigerator.

COOKING HEAT

The most important difference between cooking on a barbecue and on your stove is that the level of heat is not automatic, nor the same all over the charcoal 'bed'. Handle your fire so that you get the right degree of heat for your type of cooking. When the charcoal is burning well, spread it in an even layer over the fire-pan with tongs, and leave it to 'settle' for a few minutes before cooking. Test the heat by carefully holding your hand at meat level above the fire. If you can hold it there for 4 seconds without discomfort before having to pull it away, the temperature is probably about 275°F/140°C and you can start spit-roasting. If you can only hold it above the fire for 2 seconds, the temperature is probably about 325°F/160°C and suitable for grilling. Remember that on most barbecues you can alter the degree of cooking heat by raising or lowering the grill, or by opening or closing the damper.

However carefully you have trimmed the meat of fat, drips inevitably fall into the fire, making it flare up. Douse flare-ups when they occur with a small sprinkling of water; they will burn the food.

If the fire cools off during the last part of your grilling or roasting time, raise the grill if possible and flick off any white ash with a poker. Then give it a good pump or two with a pair of bellows, or just from a good pair of lungs, to cheer it up.

OPEN GRILLING

Grilling is the most usual kind of barbecue cooking, and steak is the meat which everyone thinks of barbecuing first. To Australians, Americans and South Africans, barbecued food really just means charcoal-grilled beefsteaks. However, other foods can be every bit as good, and the same simple cooking rules apply to them all.

Lamb and pork are particularly good when barbecue-grilled, either in large flat pieces or as steak and chops. Spare ribs, ham and thick gammon rashers are tasty treats. Veal is generally rather a dry meat for its price although cheap bits and trimmings make good Vealburgers (page 59). Treat it like poultry. Grill the other butcher's meats like beef.

Poultry, game birds, rabbit, hare and fish can all be grilled successfully. Venison can be good if marinated. Sausages and burgers are quick and easy to barbecue-grill and always popular.

Use prime cuts

Don't expect a cheap cut to give you tender, juicy meat; use prime cuts of top-quality meat for barbecue grilling. The cooking times are so short that tough meat will stay tough, so will elderly poultry and game.

If you can't afford fillet, rump or sirloin steak you can use chuck steak, but marinate it well first (page 30) and beat it flat with a mallet.

Oily fish such as mackerel, herring, trout or salmon grill better than white fish, which dries out easily.

Marinate

Marinating the meat will help a lot to tenderise cheaper cuts; so-called meat tenderisers don't do the trick. Take the trouble to make a natural marinade if you can, but if not, use a packeted marinade 'mix' and 'help' it with the end of a bottle of wine or extra long soaking.

Size of portions

The best thickness for grilling portions of meat or fish is 1–1½ in/2.5–3.5 cm. Have chops and steaks with bone in cut to this thickness, and steaks without bone if people will grill their own helpings. A tougher cut of boneless meat will be more juicy if cooked in a large, flat piece slowly and sliced after grilling. It cooks more quickly too than 'staggered' individual steaks on a small barbecue. A lamb joint can be split and boned, and laid in a flat thin 'sheet' on the grill (page 38).

Small chickens and game birds can be split lengthways, larger ones quartered; solid turkey meat can be sliced.

Cook small fish whole (but cleaned!); cut large ones into steaks like meat. If you want to grill fish fillets or fish fingers, cook them in a double-sided hinged grill. (For quick cooking, you can split whole fish like kippers and cook them the same way.)

Preparing the food

Trim excess fat off the edges of chops; it may cause flare-ups. Snip the edges of thin steaks, chops, cutlets, slices and rashers to prevent them curling during cooking. Unless well marinated, brush the food with oil or melted butter, but do not season it; salt leaches out the juices of meat or poultry and makes it tough. Brush lamb, poultry and veal with plenty of fat.

Cooking the food

The centre of the fire and the grill should both be very hot before you start grilling. As a rule, the grill should be 4–5 in/10–12.5 cm above the fire. When both are really hot, oil the bars of the grill, and lay the food on it. Remember that the centre of the fire will always be hotter than the edges, so place larger items in the centre, and smaller ones around it. Do not crowd them; leave plenty of space around them for turning them.

If you want a well-browned outside crust on your food, and have a movable grill, you can start the cooking with the grill only 2 in/5 cm above the fire, and sear the surface of the food on both sides, then raise the grill to finish the cooking.

As a rule, grill steaks or chops on one side until the top surface is beaded with bubbles, then turn them, and continue turning often until the meat is done as you like it. (See chart overleaf.) Baste meat or fish well when turning it, either with a marinade or 'baste', or just with melted butter or oil.

Never turn meat, poultry or other food or test them for readiness by piercing them with a fork or skewer. You will dry them out. Turn them with tongs or with a broad spatula.

Baste with a brush or washing-up mop, not from a jug, to avoid flare-ups.

Season pre-sliced steaks, chops etc, as soon as they are cooked, and add any savoury butter or other topping, relish or sauce. Carve a large piece of steak or other joint on a board and distribute slices. Any condiments, vegetables and salads should be close at hand on the serving table so that the meat can be dressed and eaten right away.

Cooking times

The times given below are only approximate. Much depends on the heat of your fire, draughts, the height of the grill, where the food is placed on it, and on how efficient your barbecue is.

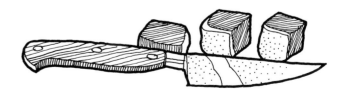

Food	Size/Weight	Minutes on each side		Notes
		Rare	Well done	
Beef				
Steak	1 in/2.5 cm thick	5	8	Best rare
	1½ in/3.5 cm thick	6	10	
	2 in/5 cm thick	9	15–18	
Kebab	Whole skewer	6–7	10–12	
Burger	1 in/2.5 cm thick	4	7	
Lamb				
Chop or steak	1 in/2.5 cm thick	5	8	Liked rare on the
Chop or steak	1½ in/3.5 cm thick	6	9	Continent
Kebab	Whole skewer		10–12	
Whole leg	Spitted	30–35 per lb		
Pork				
Chop	1 in/2.5 cm thick		13	Cook well
Spare rib	Whole rack		35–45	Turn often
Veal				
Chop	1 in/2.5 cm thick		9–11	Cook well
Burger	½ in/1 cm thick		6	
Kebab	Whole skewer		15	Cook well, turn often
Poultry/Game				
Chicken	Portion		20–30	
Duck	Portion		20–30	
Chicken	Whole spitted per lb.		30	
Duck	Split per lb.		25	
Game bird	Split per lb.		25	
Ham				
Slices	1 in/2.5 cm thick		13–18	
Sausages				
Large			15	Don't prick, moisten
Chipolata			12	

Food	Size/Weight	Minutes on each side Rare	Well done	Notes
Fish				
Whole	*per 8 oz./225 g.*	6		*Do not overcook any fish or it will be dry*
Split or steak	*1 in/2.5 cm thick*	3–5		
Fillet (thick)				
or whole sardines		6		
Fillet (thin)		3–5		

Variations

You can do a dozen and one different things to barbecued-grilled foods to vary them. You can stick herbs in them, rub spices into them, beat them, smother them with a savoury sauce, or weigh them down with a pat of chilled savoury butter or pâté. Some of these flavouring variations sound like torture, and some are. By all means have your favourite savoury butter or sauce at hand for people to use if they wish but don't insist on their use or try to make any barbecue food a set-piece. The pleasure of a barbecue anywhere in the world lies in simple eating. Most people enjoy it just as much or more if they have a plain but well-grilled piece of steak or chop without any fancy extras at all.

COOKING IN FOIL

Cooking in foil packets is an excellent way to barbecue small items such as thin cutlets, lamb's kidneys or fish fillets which would otherwise dry out. The food can be packed and seasoned in the kitchen ahead of time, leaving nothing to do outdoors except put the packets on the grill.

Use a generous piece of foil for each package. Oil or grease it lightly all over, then lay the seasoned and herbed food in the centre of the greased foil, and do up the package securely like a parcel. The parcel must not let juices seep out but try to avoid making thick double folds which may make heat penetrate the foil unevenly.

Foil-wrapped packets can either be cooked on the grill rack or be placed directly on the hot coals at the edge of the fire.

One of the special merits of foil parcels is that they hold the heat for a long time; so they can be cooked before open grilling begins and can be used to feed anyone who has to wait his turn at the barbecue, or who arrives late. Generally, too, if they are not used, they can be frozen just as they are, for an ordinary meal later.

KEBAB OR SKEWER COOKING

Kebabs are known world-wide by various names. Whatever they are called, they consist of small pieces of food threaded on metal or bamboo skewers or wires and then grilled. Usually two or more foods are combined to create colour and flavour contrasts.

Choose foods for skewer cooking which will not soften or flake when cooked; for instance choose firm-fleshed fish. Small meatballs made of seasoned mince are a popular and quickly-cooked kebab item as a change from solid meat or fish cubes. They should be bound with egg or crumbs and not too fatty because as the fat melts they may fall apart and drop off the skewer into the fire.

For each skewer assortment, choose foods which will cook in the same length of time. No one wants to eat assorted 'bits' some of which are overcooked while others are still half raw.

The foods should be cubed, then seasoned or marinated. They can then be put on the skewers ahead of time.

The skewers or wires should be lightly oiled before the food is put on them, and the food items should also be lightly oiled just before grilling.

Take care to put the skewer through the centre of each cube. If one side is heavier than the other, the food item will swivel round on the skewer so that only the heavier side gets cooked.

If all the skewer items will cook in the same time, you can if you prefer put the various 'bits' in separate bowls on the cooks' table so that each person can fill his own skewer with the items he prefers. Put a jug of oil and a brush beside them.

As a rule, skewers take a bit longer to cook than solid pieces of meat and fish. (See chart page 22.) Remember to keep them well basted to prevent them drying out.

SPIT-ROASTING

Spit-roasting is a bit more work than the other kinds of barbecue cooking but is always rewarding.

Meat joints or whole poultry or game birds should be marinated and tied into a neat shape securely. Thin flat pieces of meat such as breast of lamb can be sprinkled with stuffing all over the flesh side, then rolled up and tied tightly. Bone-in joints are better boned to make balancing on the spit easier. The hollow left by the bone can be stuffed. Small meat items such as lamb's or pig's hearts can also be stuffed and spit-roasted whole.

Skewer barding fat or fat streaky bacon over a joint covering it; then tie the joint with string at 2 in/5 cm intervals to keep the fat in place and to keep the joint in a neat shape. The skewers can then be removed.

Put the meat or bird on the spit before starting the fire, and rotate it to make sure it is evenly balanced. Spit a joint centrally through its longest part. Spit birds parallel to their backbones bringing the end of the spit out between legs and tail. Once balanced, keep the meat aside, still on the spit, until ready to barbecue.

Use a meat thermometer if possible when spit-roasting if you want all the meat fully cooked before serving. If you like, however, you can carve the outside slices of a joint still on the spit (like a doner kebab, page 52) before it is fully cooked through, and leave the half-raw meat exposed, to go on cooking.

The fire should be near the back of the barbecue. Place a drip pan in front, under the meat, taking care that there are no hot coals or ashes under the pan. Baste the meat with the pan juices and with butter or oil. Also baste with Barbecue Baste (page 30) if you use it, for the last 15–30 minutes of the cooking time.

KETTLE COOKING

Any barbecue cooking method can be used with success in a barbecue kettle – a barbecue with a lid (page 10); although spit-roasting is not used because even large items such as a turkey can simply be placed on the grill, and the lid closed. It then holds in the heat, so that the food cooks in the same way as in an oven.

If you have a kettle and use this method, you can also 'smoke-cook' the food by adding wood chips to the charcoal, or 'steam-cook' it by standing a pan of water on the grill beside it. Steam-cooking helps to keep large items of food moist and succulent.

For closed-kettle cooking, use the same roasting times that you would use in an ordinary oven, as soon as the fire has really got going.

GAS-FIRED COOKING

Gas-fired barbecues usually have two controls, high and low, giving you a choice of easily-managed heats. You will probably find that you can cook most foods on the lower heat, and use the high heat mostly for 'instant' browning.

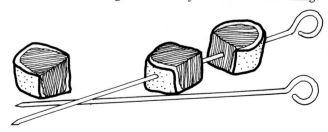

PLANNING YOUR BARBECUE

However informal, a barbecue meal must be planned to some extent. If it is just a Sunday brunch barbecue for the family, you may only have to thaw pre-cut steaks and Barbecue Baste from the freezer, check over your bag of barbecue equipment (pages 14–16) and prepare a salad, a bowl of fresh fruit and vacuum flask of coffee. An evening party for guests however needs fairly careful pre-planning.

Although informal, your barbecue setting must be convenient. No one enjoys stumbling around in the half-dark or trying to grill their food on an ill-lit smoky fire. Both the scene and the food must also be suited to the type and the number of guests. Teenagers will like finger-foods such as burgers and chicken drumsticks, with disco music to dance to; older guests invited formally may enjoy a foreign setting atmosphere with appropriate food from the recipes in this book. Both the 'props' and menu must be planned ahead, and the dishes prepared.

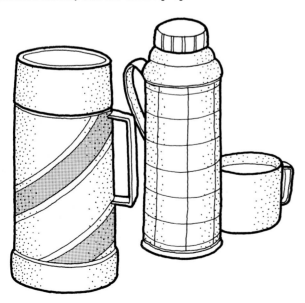

THE COOKING AND SERVING AREAS

Safety and convenience are overriding in deciding where to site a portable barbecue (or barbecues for a large party). It must be fairly near the kitchen for fetching and carrying, and near enough to a power socket to run an extension lead from it if you use any electrical appliances. Preferably it should be near the dustbin too. For safety features see page 17.

Having sited your barbecue, plan to set up two trestle or similar tables, one near the cooking area (the cooks' table) for raw foods, the other further away for salads, desserts, condiments, plates and so on (the serving table). With these allocated, spread the rest of your scene. A bar table is essential, but put it a little way away from the food areas, so that guests spread out. Ideally, place it close to the 'entrance' to your barbecue scene so that people will see it as soon as they arrive. Arrange to have a few up-ended wooden boxes covered with plastic traycloths scattered about to serve as tables, and put plates of 'nibblers' (page 31) on them at party-time if not handing them round; this, too, will save crowding.

Strategically placed rubbish bags or bins are a 'must' both for safety and to save you clearing up a litter of used napkins, disposable mugs and stray bones next day.

Another essential for any barbecue party is something to sit on. Groundsheets and cushions do for young people, but have some garden chairs for older guests. Deck chairs are not a good idea.

The right lighting is very important. The bar, cooks' table, serving table and the barbecue itself must all be well lit, either by lights left on in the house or by spotlights. Again, safety and convenience are more important than romantic gloom. Decorative lighting should at least let guests find their way about without stumbling over stray cushions. The house lights will usually make an attractive background. Fairy lights strung between trees can be appealing at the darker end of the garden. Large torches swathed in greenery or coloured flares on sticks can 'stand in' for Hawaiian flaming torches in a south sea island 'scene'; storm lanterns will add to a camp-fire or 'wild western' atmosphere. Use nightlights or candles in tins with holes punched in them to mark steps or the edge of a driveway. Do not use naked candles, however romantic they look; people wandering about, eating and chatting, can too easily knock them over, and any draught may blow them out, leaving the scene dark and smelling of guttering wax.

COOKS OR SERVE-YOURSELF
In countries such as South Africa where most people are practised barbecuers, guests take their own foods from the cooks' table, make up their own kebabs, and grill their own food. But you need a large cooking area, and a lot of equipment such as tongs and skewers. If you will have more than a small group of guests, and certainly if you plan to spit-roast, you should collect a team of two or three cooks and handers-round ahead of time, and brief them on what you plan to serve. Ask a responsible person to act as barman.

PLANNING THE MENU
Quantities
The two golden rules in planning barbecue food are 'Keep It Simple' and 'Make It Ample'. Don't be beguiled into serving three or four different kebabs, it will only lead to confusion at the cooks' table or grill as guests peer to see if they've got the kind they want. Except at a children's party, there is no need to serve both burgers and sausages. One minced and two or three solid meat offerings are usually enough, making one a poultry grill. Salads, dips and relishes should likewise not be too numerous – but don't stint them. Appetites are whetted by fresh air.

Reckon on serving 6–8 oz./175–225 g. lean meat without bone per person, or 8–12 oz./225–340 g. fat or spit-roasted meat. If you serve chops or spare ribs, allow an extra 4–8 oz./100–225 g. per person. Most people will only eat one baked potato (page 65) but double your usual quantity of salad and allow 2 bread rolls or pitta breads (page 72–73) per person. Serve only a few kinds of drinks, say mulled ale or cider in cool weather, a cold punch in hot

weather plus beer or one table wine and two kinds of soft drinks. Get the beer or wine on sale or return if possible, so that you have a generous stock in hand. Be generous with coffee too; expect everyone to drink a third of a pint at least.
What to serve
Make yourself a menu, keeping in mind the numbers you must serve, what you can afford, and what facilities you have for storing made-ahead items. Choose at least one item which you can pre-cook in the oven such as spare ribs or which can easily and quickly be oven-baked if 'rain stops play'. Have a backstop too, in case numbers grow unexpectedly. Extra sausages or chops can be frozen and served to the family if not used. Commercially frozen burgers or similar foods in packets are compact and quickly thawed.

Remember that a balanced meal and a refreshing one must include at least one leafy salad or fresh fruit as well as breads and meats. Another thing to remember is that you must try to keep cold foods such as salads cold until the last moment, and that any hot baste or sauce may need to be kept hot balanced on the barbecue so must be in a solid, hard-to-spill container. Beg, borrow or steal enough vacuum flasks and food flasks for your needs, and at least one insulated bag which can be turned into a portable 'fridge by putting frozen cold packs inside. Use it for keeping butter, milk and salads cold until the moment of serving. Don't forget either that you will need ice for drinks in warm weather so freeze plenty of ice cubes in advance to make sure you don't run out.

PLANNING A SPECIAL EVENING
Just to make your barbecue a little different, why not choose a theme and plan your barbecue scene and your recipes to suit. Children will love a Wild West barbecue, and a Far Eastern or Turkish-style barbecue is fun for adults. Here are some suggestions for special barbecues which should give you some ideas. Don't worry if everything is not completely authentic – it won't spoil anyone's enjoyment!

CHILDREN'S WILD WEST PARTY

If you are having a children's party, why not make it fancy dress, and give your party games a 'wild west' flavour.

For children, both the setting and the food should be kept simple. Use a bright gingham tablecloth if you have one, and enamel plates and mugs for a real 'outdoors' feel. Keep cutlery to a minimum – kids love finger food – and have plenty of kitchen paper handy to wipe greasy fingers.

A simple starter will keep the children occupied while you are barbecuing, but don't serve too much and ruin their appetites for the main course.

Steak and Texan Barbecued Roast are authentic, but rather expensive for large numbers, and children will enjoy burgers and sausages just as much. Choose one recipe for each, plus a kebab, and either a chicken or fish dish if you want extra variety. Tomato sauce and Barbecue Relish go well with burgers.

Corn and jacket potatoes are the best vegetables. If you want a salad, keep it simple and refreshing.

Serve a spicy dessert, or just fresh fruit.

Stock up on the children's favourite soft drinks and serve Spiced Tomato Juice.

Cold starter
Piccalilli Dip and Creamy Onion–Cucumber Dip with Dunkers.
Hot starter
Soup sprinkled with grated cheese.
Meat/Fish
Texan Barbecued Roast, Steak, Mississippi Grill. Or Hey Presto Burgers, Barbecued Bangers and Mississippi Grill. Marinated Chicken or Florida Fish Fillets are other choices.
Vegetables
Jacket potatoes and Bacon-Wrapped Corn or Husked Indian Corn. Green salad with Blue Cheese Dressing.
Desserts
Gingerbread or fruit.
Drinks
Spiced Tomato Juice and a selection of soft drinks.

ORIENTAL BARBECUE

If you want to try a really different barbecue, select some Far Eastern dishes. You could use flaming torches from the barbecue shop to decorate and light the garden, and choose spicy kebabs and fish dishes.

Spicy Mushrooms makes a super starter, or you could serve grapefruit sprinkled with demerara sugar and toasted on the grill.

For the main course, grill some pork fillets with your favourite herbs, or a wine marinade. Kalbi-Kui is delicious and very different. A-Me'Huat, Chicken Satay or Sweet-Sour Fish Kebabs also make excellent choices, but beware of offering too many dishes.

Yellow Rice or simple boiled rice go best with these dishes, as does Bean Sprout and Fruit Salad.

Sweet barbecued fruits make a refreshing end to a delicious meal.

Serve Port-of-Call Party Punch, or wine.

Starter
Spicy Mushrooms or grapefruit with demerara sugar.
Meat/Fish
Choose from: Pork Fillets, Kalbi-Kui, A'Me-Huat, Chicken Satay and Sweet-Sour Fish Kebabs.
Vegetables
Yellow Rice or boiled rice. Bean Sprout and Fruit Salad and a plain green salad if wished.
Dessert
Sweet barbecued fruits.
Drinks
Port-of-Call Party Punch and wine.

ENOUGH FUEL?

Check over your equipment and accessories at the same time as you order the food. Refer to the check lists on pages 14–16. Make sure you have enough fuel, firelighters, cooking and serving gear. Order any special effects you want for your party, such as spotlights or canned music, at the same time.

COOKING AHEAD

Almost all your food preparation can be done ahead, as soon as meat orders arrive, or sooner in the case of breads, desserts, relishes and sauces if you have a freezer. Meat, poultry and fish can be prepared when they reach you, be portioned if suitable, and frozen or marinated as time allows. Read your chosen recipes through to see how much you can do ahead. Do remember to freeze cold packs for cold food containers well ahead, and allow enough time for thawing any frozen foods before the party.

RECIPE QUANTITIES

In this book, recipes for single items such as chops or kebabs provide one normal serving per item so I have given no serving quantity for these; just allow for extra hearty open-air appetites.

As for other dishes which may be harder to estimate, I have given the normal indoor serving quantity where it seems to be needed.

ON THE DAY

The barbecue, serving tables and any other furniture can be set in place early, together with the planned lighting arrangements and any music gear. In fact everything except ice, food and any made-up drinks such as punch can be laid out well ahead of time, and decorators' plastic sheets can be draped over the tables to keep off dust, flies – and rain if necessary.

Light the fire in good time (page 18) so that it is ready for cooking shortly before the guests arrive. Get any oven-cooked items which will be finished off on the barbecue into the oven in good time too.

Put a spit-roast on its spit and make sure it is properly balanced. In the kitchen, lay prepared raw meats and fish on foil-covered trays or in large shallow containers, including any made-up kebabs. Both can be put out ready for cooking a short while before the party begins. Cover both with foil, and lay a tray or oven shelf over the grilling meats; wrap a spit-roast closely.

Most other foods can also be put ready on the tables shortly before the party starts. Put breads in baskets, fruit in bowls, any cake-like desserts such as Gingerbread (page 75) on plates. Even foil-wrapped food parcels for baking 'from raw' on the barbecue can be put out ahead. So can hot soup or coffee in vacuum flasks, thin salad dressings and relishes.

The only foods you should have to handle at the last moment are items which you are oven-cooking for barbecue 'finishing', salads, butter, any buttery hot baste or sauce which may separate on standing and of course, any hot drink such as Mulled Cider (page 77). Dips and creamy salad dressings are also best kept covered and refrigerated until the last moment in their serving containers.

Cooks should be asked to come ahead of time, and to start barbecuing any spit-roast together with a few smaller items. The aroma of grilling foods will then greet your guests with good promises as soon as they arrive, even though you may not want to encourage them to eat right away.

Ask a barman too, if not a member of the family, to come ahead of time, to arrange the bar as he wants it, to handle the ice supply and be ready to serve the first guests who arrive.

Ask a helper to switch on the lights, start up the music, and get set to enjoy your barbecue yourself.

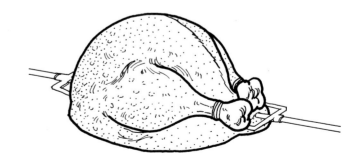

FLAVOURING YOUR FOOD

First-class meat has a fine flavour of its own but herbs, spices and seasonings can highlight it and give it new interest. They can be rubbed into the meat itself, be added to a marinade, baste or sauce, or can be put on the fire in the form of burning woods and herbs.

You can use any herbs or spices which appeal to you. There are no fixed rules as to which you should use although some herbs are traditional with particular meat dishes. Look at the recipes in the following sections as a guide to suitable choices.

Always use fresh herbs if you can, or good quality dried herbs in jars from a store with a quick turnover. Choose a well-known brand because this, too, is a guarantee of quality; a big firm will probably market all your most-needed spices too, and even supply a rack for them which can be a blessing.

Besides single herbs and spices, most large firms supply ready-mixed combinations: lemon and pepper seasoning for instance, and various barbecue seasonings.

Try them, cautiously, on one small item at first. You may find you like them or that you prefer your own individual 'mixes'.

The same goes for the various marinade and barbecue sauce 'mixes' on the market. If you use them, try adding a touch of your own such as a spoonful of wine or a scrap of squeezed garlic.

If you decide to try barbecue-burning woods and herbs, remember that they will scent the whole fire, so be cautious if you have various different meats and fish items on the grill. You don't want them all to have the same character. If you are barbecuing just one or two different foods, these mixtures can be a delight sending their fragrant aroma into the air as well as scenting the food itself. They are distributed by Weber Distribution Ltd., Unit 7, Bridge Street Mill, Witney, Oxon, OX8 6YA.

Get the most out of the simplest spices. Sea salt has more vigour than table salt, the slightly unusual spicy note of mignonette pepper can be delicious, and there are now excellent ready-mixed herb and spice mustards available in most supermarkets.

BASTES AND MARINADES

Marinades tenderise your meat, poultry or other food and give it enough moisture to stand the heat of the barbecue coals. Basting helps to keep it moist while it cooks, and adds flavour to its succulence.

Barbecue Baste

U.S.A.

INGREDIENTS	Imperial	Metric	American
Pure corn oil	*¼ pt.*	*150 ml.*	*⅔ cup*
Red wine	*¼ pt.*	*150 ml.*	*⅔ cup*
Orange juice	*¼ pt.*	*150 ml.*	*⅔ cup*
Garlic clove, peeled	*1*	*1*	*1*
Onion, finely chopped	*2 tbsp.*	*2 tbsp.*	*2 tbsp.*
Parsley, chopped	*1 tsp.*	*1 tsp.*	*1 tsp.*
Pinch of ground coriander			
Salt and ground black pepper			

For red meats, steaks, chops, burgers, sausages, etc.

Put the liquids in a saucepan, squeeze the garlic over them, and add the onion and parsley. Stir round, bring to the boil and remove from the heat. Strain into a jug and season to taste. Use for basting foods while cooking if they have not been marinated and have no special baste of their own.

For white meats, chicken and fish, use lemon juice instead of wine and water instead of orange juice.

Basic Wine Marinade

International

INGREDIENTS	Imperial	Metric	American
Small onion, skinned and sliced	*1*	*1*	*1*
Parsley stalks, chopped	*6*	*6*	*6*
Sprig of dried thyme			
Bay leaf	*½*	*½*	*½*
Strip of lemon peel	*1*	*1*	*1*
Salt and ground black pepper			
Red or white wine (see method)	*8 fl. oz.*	*225 ml.*	*1 cup*
White wine vinegar	*1 tbsp.*	*1 tbsp.*	*1 tbsp.*
Corn oil	*2 tbsp.*	*2 tbsp.*	*2 tbsp.*

For meat, game, poultry or fish.

Scatter the onion over the bottom of a glass or earthenware dish. Tie the herbs and lemon peel loosely in a piece of cloth and put with the onion. Add the food and season it well. Pour the liquids over. Marinate fish (white wine) for at least 30 minutes, white meat or poultry (white wine) 2–4 hours, red meat or game (red wine) 6–8 hours or overnight. Turn food over sometimes so that all parts are soaked. Strain if using as a baste or sauce.

There are hundreds of other marinades. This is a simple basic one. Add fennel or dill seeds to the herb bundle for fish if you like, and substitute lemon juice for vinegar. Add a few juniper berries and 2 whole cloves to the herb bundle for game.

Makes enough to soak 2 lb./1 kg. food.

STARTERS

Although your barbecue entertaining should be as simple as possible, one or two 'easy-to-eat' starters are essential. Even small barbecued items take time to cook, and people, especially children, get restless when they're hungry and smell the good cooking.

Mugs of warming soup are excellent on a chilly evening. At other times the best starter of all is not a set-piece dish but just a choice of raw and blanched vegetables arranged in a picture book pattern on one or two trays. They're easy to pick up and eat while waiting one's turn to barbecue, and their fresh crispness contrasts well with the charcoal-grilled foods. You'll find that people will come back and pick up 'nibblers' between eating barbecued items too, so prepare plenty.

Offer a choice of dips with the vegetables. People come back to these as well, and use them instead of a sauce with their barbecued foods or as salad dressings.

Have one or two small dishes of other 'nibblers' around. Salted nuts, crisps, olives or cheese straws are always popular or, for a slightly more solid 'nibbler' savoury pastry fingers.

Scandinavian Pea Soup

Denmark   Illustration page 75

INGREDIENTS	Imperial	Metric	American
Butter	1 oz.	25 g.	2 tbsp.
Streaky bacon rashers without rind, chopped	2 oz.	50 g.	1/4 cup
Large onion, chopped	1	1	1
Yellow split peas, washed	4 oz.	100 g.	4 oz.
Chicken stock	1½ pts.	900 ml.	4 cups (scant)
Salt and ground black pepper			

Melt the butter in a heavy stewpan, and fry the chopped bacon and onion until soft. Add the peas and stock and season well. Cover and simmer for 1½ hours or pressure cook for 11 minutes. Put the peas in batches in an electric blender with a little stock and process until smooth. Mix with the rest of the stock. Reheat when needed and pour into a large vacuum flask. Seal securely. Serve in mugs.

Serves 4.

Dunkers

International   Illustration page 33

INGREDIENTS

Cauliflower sprigs	*Choose from these or other*
Salt	*firm 'dippable' vegetables.*
Cucumber	*Add radishes, button*
Inner stalks of celery	*mushrooms or olives if you*
Fennel stems	*can be bothered to stick*
Small carrots	*wooden toothpicks into them*
Asparagus spears, cooked	*as 'carriers'.*

Blanch cauliflower sprigs in boiling salted water for 3–4 minutes. Quarter cucumber lengthways, scrape celery and fennel if needed. Cut cucumber, celery, fennel and carrot into 3 in/7.5 cm lengths. Arrange vegetables in lines or clumps on a big platter with contrasting colours side by side. There's no need to season them if you serve them with any of the following five delicious dips.

Piccalilli Dip

U.S.A.

INGREDIENTS	Imperial	Metric	American
Piccalilli	4 oz.	100 g.	1/2 cup
Natural yoghurt	1/4 pt.	150 ml.	2/3 cup
Salt and pepper			

Chop the piccalilli, beat in the yoghurt and season.

Taramasalata

Greece   Illustration page 33

INGREDIENTS	Imperial	Metric	American
White bread slices *without crusts*	12	12	12
Milk	½ pt.	300 ml.	1¼ cups
Smoked cod's roe, *skinned*	6 oz.	175 g.	6 oz.
Onion, skinned and *chopped*	¼	¼	¼
Juice of 2 lemons			
Oil	16 tbsp.	16 tbsp.	1 cup

Soak the bread in the milk. Squeeze it dry. Put it in an electric blender with the smoked roe, onion and lemon juice. Blend until smooth; still blending, trickle in the oil until the mixture becomes smooth and creamy. Refrigerate until well chilled. Serve hot Pitta (page 72) with this dip as well as vegetable Dunkers.

Spicy Tomato Dip

Southern Europe   Illustration page 33

INGREDIENTS	Imperial	Metric	American
Full-fat soft *('cream') cheese*	4 oz.	100 g.	½ cup
Milk	1 tbsp.	1 tbsp.	1 tbsp.
Tomato chutney	2 tsp.	2 tsp.	2 tsp.
Lemon juice	1 tsp.	1 tsp.	1 tsp.
Tabasco	3–4 drops	3–4 drops	3–4 drops
Salt and black pepper			

Process all the ingredients together in a blender. Adjust the seasoning.

Creamy Onion-Cucumber Dip

U.S.A.   Illustration page 33

INGREDIENTS	Imperial	Metric	American
Full-fat soft *('cream') cheese*	4 oz.	100 g.	½ cup
Milk	1 tbsp.	1 tbsp.	1 tbsp.
Cream of Onion Soup Mix *(dried, from pkt)*	1 tbsp.	1 tbsp.	1 tbsp.
Cucumber, diced	1 in piece	5 cm piece	1 in piece

Process the cheese, milk and dried soup mix together in a blender. Leave to stand for 15 minutes. Fold in the cucumber.

Smoked Mackerel Dip

Scandinavia   Illustration page 33

INGREDIENTS	Imperial	Metric	American
Smoked mackerel fillets, *skinned*	8 oz.	225 g.	½ lb.
Cottage cheese	4 oz.	113 g.	½ cup
Single cream or natural *yoghurt*	6 fl. oz.	175 ml.	¾ cup
Lemon juice	4 tsp.	4 tsp.	4 tsp.
Pinch of grated nutmeg			
Pinch of cayenne pepper			
Margarine, melted	4 oz.	100 g.	½ cup
Salt and pepper (optional)			

Process all the ingredients in an electric blender. Add extra cream or yoghurt if needed to give a smooth creamy dipping consistency. Season if you wish.

Spicy Mushrooms

England

INGREDIENTS	Imperial	Metric	American
Button mushrooms	*8 oz.*	*225 g.*	*½ lb.*
Ginger wine	*½ pt.*	*350 ml.*	*1¼ cups*
Brown sugar	*4 tsp.*	*4 tsp.*	*4 tsp.*
Small honeydew melon			
(optional)	*1*	*1*	*1*

Days ahead of time if you like, make your spiced mushrooms. Put a 1 lb/450 g. jam jar with a lug-top lid to heat gently in the oven. Put the mushrooms, wine and sugar in a saucepan. Bring slowly to the boil, turn down the heat and cover. Simmer gently for 10 minutes; the wine should be well reduced and syrupy. Take the jar out of the oven, stand it on stout paper and pour the mushroom mixture into it. Put on the lid loosely and leave to cool. Screw on the lid tightly when cold, and keep in a cool place until needed.

These spiced mushrooms are a super alternative to olives. Serve them just as they are, as a 'nibbler' on cocktail sticks or as a relish with barbecued meats.

To make a more formal starter for people waiting to barbecue, cut open the melon, remove the seeds, and cut the flesh into small balls. Toss the balls with an equal quantity of drained spiced mushrooms. Serve in small saucer glasses or bowls.

Serves 4.

Dunkers, page 31, Taramasalata (*left*), Smoked Mackerel Dip (*right*), Creamy Onion-Cucumber Dip (*top*), Spicy Tomato Dip (*centre*), page 32 and Pitta Bread, page 72

Ham and Cheese Fingers

England

INGREDIENTS	Imperial	Metric	American
For the pastry			
Flour	8 oz.	225 g.	2 cups
Margarine	4 oz.	100 g.	½ cup
Cold water	2 tbsp.	2 tbsp.	2 tbsp.
For the filling			
Ham or gammon, finely shredded	4 oz.	100 g.	½ cup
Soft white breadcrumbs	2 oz.	50 g.	1 cup
Tomato paste	1 tsp.	1 tsp.	1 tsp.
Sprinkling of dry mustard			
Grated cheese	4 oz.	100 g.	¼ cup
Beaten egg			

Sift the flour into a bowl. Rub in the fat until the mixture resembles breadcrumbs. Bind to a pliant pastry with the water. Knead lightly, then roll out on a floured surface into a 12 in/30 cm square. Cut the square into 2 equal rectangles. Chill for 15 minutes. Heat the oven to 425°F/220°C/Gas Mark 7.

Place one rectangle on a damped baking sheet. Blend thoroughly the ham or gammon, breadcrumbs, tomato paste and mustard. Spread on the pastry on the baking sheet, leaving ½ in/1 cm of the edge bare all round. Scatter the cheese on top. Brush the edges of the pastry with egg, and fit on the second piece of pastry to make a lid. Seal the edges. Brush the top of the pastry with egg. Bake for 25–30 minutes. Cool, then cut into fingers, trimming off excess pastry at the edges.

Makes 12 fingers.

These pastry snacks make excellent nibblers for barbe-queuers. They can even be used as dunkers.

Cheese Straws

England

INGREDIENTS	Imperial	Metric	American
Butter, softened	4 oz.	100 g.	½ cup
Flour	4 oz.	100 g.	1 cup
Cheddar cheese, finely grated	4 oz.	100 g.	1 cup
Salt	¼ tsp.	¼ tsp.	¼ tsp.

Beat the butter into the flour with a rotary or electric beater, then beat in the grated cheese and seasonings. Shape the dough into two equal-sized balls with lightly floured hands. Chill for 45 minutes.

On a floured surface, roll out one ball of dough into a rectangle ¼ in/1.25 cm thick. Leave the other ball chilled. Cut the rolled-out dough into fingers 3 in/7.5 cm long and about ⅓ in/2 cm wide. Repeat using the remaining dough. Bake at 350°F/180°C/Gas Mark 4 for 15–17 minutes until light gold. Cool on the sheets. Serve cold.

Makes about 5 dozen straws.

MEATS – BEEF, LAMB AND PORK

Texan Barbecued Roast
U.S.A.

INGREDIENTS	Imperial	Metric	American
Red wine vinegar	4 fl. oz.	120 ml.	½ cup
Oil	4 fl. oz.	120 ml.	½ cup
Worcestershire sauce	2 fl. oz.	60 ml.	¼ cup
Tomato ketchup	4 fl. oz.	120 ml.	½ cup
Salt	3 tsp.	3 tsp.	3 tsp.
Pepper	1 tsp.	1 tsp.	1 tsp.
Cayenne pepper to taste			
Beef chuck	3 lb.	1.5 kg.	3 lb.

Heat all the ingredients except the meat until on the boil. Remove from the heat. Brush the meat all over with the sauce. Heat the oven to 250°F/120°C/Gas Mark ½. Put the meat on a rack in a roasting tin, and place in the oven for 3 hours, basting frequently with the sauce. Transfer the meat to the barbecue, and continue cooking, turning as needed, until it has an authentic smoky taste and well-browned surface. See chart, page 22. Let the meat 'rest' for 5–10 minutes before carving.

Genuine Texans like the larger cuts of cheaper meat almost as much as steaks because the meat slices are moister as well as cheaper. More often than not, they pre-cook joints in the oven before barbecuing them to make sure they are well cooked through, especially when only a family-sized barbecue is being used.

Serves 6–8.

Texan Barbecued Roast with Kidney Kebabs, page 49, and Double-Covered Onions, page 64

Piquant Chops

International

INGREDIENTS	Imperial	Metric	American
For the Piquant Butter			
Butter, softened	8 oz.	225 g.	1 cup
Capers, drained and chopped	3 tbsp.	3 tbsp.	3 tbsp.
Soft brown sugar	2 tsp.	2 tsp.	2 tsp.
For the chops			
Best end lamb chops (or see below)	8	8	8
Pepper			
Butter	8 oz.	225 g.	1 cup
Clear honey	2 tbsp.	2 tbsp.	2 tbsp.
White wine vinegar	2 tbsp.	2 tbsp.	2 tbsp.
Salt			
Rosemary sprigs (optional)	8	8	8

Make the Piquant Butter by mixing all the ingredients thoroughly. Shape into 16 flat round pats and chill.

Trim about 1 in/2.5 cm of the meat off the bone ends of the chops. Rub pepper lightly into the meat on both sides. Heat the butter, honey and vinegar in a small saucepan until the butter melts. Stir well. Brush both sides of the chops with this glaze. Cook the chops on the barbecue for 8–10 minutes on each side, basting well with glaze while cooking. Season lightly. If helpers are serving ask them to make a small slit in one side of each chop, and insert a rosemary sprig. Serve the chops topped with the chilled pats of Piquant Butter.

To vary, you could use chump or loin chops, and make Mint Butter instead of Piquant Butter. Instead of capers and brown sugar, use 1½ tbsp./20 ml. chopped fresh mint, 2 tsp./10 ml. caster sugar and 2 tsp./10 ml. each boiling water and vinegar.

Piquant Chops with Savoury Burgers, page 55

South Sea Spare Ribs

Polynesia

INGREDIENTS	Imperial	Metric	American
For the marinade			
Soy sauce	6 tbsp.	6 tbsp.	6 tbsp.
Red wine	4 tbsp.	4 tbsp.	4 tbsp.
Tomato ketchup (catsup)	6 tbsp.	6 tbsp.	6 tbsp.
Pineapple juice (unsweetened)	5 tbsp.	5 tbsp.	5 tbsp.
Basil leaves, dried	1 tbsp.	1 tbsp.	1 tbsp.
Sage leaves (fresh if possible)	4	4	4
Oil	8 fl. oz.	225 ml.	1 cup
Pinch of black pepper			
For the spare ribs			
Pork spare ribs, separated	3½ lb.	1.6 kg.	3½ lb.

Mix all the marinade ingredients in a bowl which will hold the spare ribs. Marinate the spare ribs in the mixture overnight, turning occasionally. Drain and dry well. Put in a greased baking tin in 1 or 2 layers. Bake at 350°F/180°C/Gas Mark 4 for 25–30 minutes on each side, basting often with the marinade. Drain the ribs. Transfer to the barbecue, and turn over the hot coals for a few minutes until glazed and with a broiled flavour. The meat between the ribs should still be juicy.

Butterflied Lamb

New Zealand   Illustration far right

INGREDIENTS	Imperial	Metric	American
For the marinade			
Lemon juice	4 tbsp.	60 ml.	4 tbsp.
Dry white wine	¼ pt.	150 ml.	⅔ cup
Worcestershire sauce	2 tbsp.	2 tbsp.	2 tbsp.
Oil	2 tbsp.	2 tbsp.	2 tbsp.
Garlic cloves, crushed	2	2	2
Dried herbs (basil marjoram, rosemary)	1 tsp. each	1 tsp. each	1 tsp. each
Salt and pepper			
For the meat			
Leg of lamb, boned	2½ lb.	1.1 kg.	2½ lb.

Mix the marinade ingredients together in a plastic bag. Open the boned leg out flat in the shape of a butterfly. Lay it in the marinade, close the plastic bag securely, and leave the meat to marinate for 24 hours. Turn it over from time to time.

Lay the meat on the barbecue and cook for about 30 minutes on each side. To give it extra flavour, sprinkle burning herbs on the charcoal while cooking (see page 29). Let the meat 'rest' for 5–10 minutes before slicing it.

This is an excellent way to do any small joint if you have no barbecue spit. Remember that even half a small leg of pork will need longer cooking than lamb, so only tackle it if you can start your barbecue fire well ahead of time.

Serves 6–8.

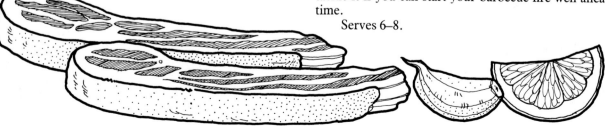

Minted Lamb Steaks

New Zealand

INGREDIENTS	Imperial	Metric	American
Leg bone lamb steaks,			
1½ in/4 cm thick	*6*	*6*	*6*
Melted butter	*2 oz.*	*50 g.*	*5 tbsp.*
Fresh mint, chopped	*2 tbsp.*	*30 ml.*	*2 tbsp.*
Salt and pepper			

Trim the steaks. Mix the melted butter and mint, and sprinkle on the steaks. Cook the steaks on the barbecue until done to your liking (see chart, page 22). Sprinkle with butter and mint when turning.

Serve with a salad containing sharp fruits. New Zealanders team chopped fresh peaches, paper-thin apple slices dipped in lemon juice and sliced kiwi fruits with finely shredded white cabbage lightly dressed with mayonnaise.

Lamb leg bone steaks make an excellent alternative to beef steak. For a classic barbecued flavour, try them marinated as in the Honey-Marinated Lamb or Pork Steaks (page 40).

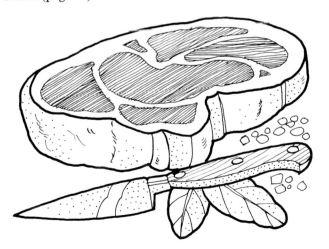

Butterflied Lamb and Minted Lamb Steaks

Honey-Marinated Lamb or Pork Steaks

International

INGREDIENTS	Imperial	Metric	American
Tomato ketchup	*1/4 pt.*	*150 ml.*	*2/3 cup*
Clear honey	*2 tbsp.*	*2 tbsp.*	*2 tbsp.*
Lemon juice	*2 tbsp.*	*2 tbsp.*	*2 tbsp.*
Pure corn oil	*2 tbsp.*	*2 tbsp.*	*2 tbsp.*
Worcestershire sauce	*1 tbsp.*	*1 tbsp.*	*1 tbsp.*
Lamb leg bone steaks or thick slices of pork	*4*	*4*	*4*
Tomatoes	*4*	*4*	*4*

Mix together the ketchup, honey, lemon juice, oil and Worcestershire sauce in a saucepan. Warm through, stirring until blended. Pour over the steaks in a shallow dish, and leave for 30 minutes, turning once. Cook steaks on the barbecue (see chart, page 22) using the marinade to baste them while cooking. Add the tomatoes for the last 5 minutes.

Also a good way to serve lamb or pork chops.

Kalbi-Kui (Barbecued Spare Rib Portions)

Korea — Illustration page 51

INGREDIENTS	Imperial	Metric	American
Pork spare ribs (short ribs)	*2 lb.*	*1 kg.*	*2 lb.*
Soy sauce	*5 tbsp.*	*5 tbsp.*	*5 tbsp.*
Sugar	*2 tbsp.*	*2 tbsp.*	*2 tbsp.*
Leek, finely chopped	*5 tbsp.*	*5 tbsp.*	*5 tbsp.*
Garlic, finely chopped	*2 tsp.*	*2 tsp.*	*2 tsp.*

Fresh ginger root,			
finely chopped	*1 tsp.*	*1 tsp.*	*1 tsp.*
Groundnut or sesame oil	*1½ tbsp.*	*1½ tbsp.*	*1½ tbsp.*

Ask the butcher to cut the spare ribs into 3 in/7.5 cm portions. Mix together all the other ingredients except the oil. Make deep slits with a knife-point all over the spare rib portions, and toss them with the marinade. Sprinkle with the oil. Leave to stand for 2 hours. Drain the portions. Then cook them on the barbecue (or in the oven), slowly, for about 30 minutes on each side, basting well while cooking. If oven-cooked, finish on the barbecue until well-crisped.

Honey-Basted Pork Chops

England

INGREDIENTS	Imperial	Metric	American
Large pork chops	6	6	6
Ground black pepper			
Clear honey, warmed	*3 tbsp.*	*3 tbsp.*	*3 tbsp.*
Dry cider	*8 fl. oz.*	*225 ml.*	*1 cup*
Powdered sage	*2 tsp.*	*2 tsp.*	*2 tsp.*

Season the chops well with pepper. Put them in a shallow dish. Mix the honey, cider and sage together and pour over the chops. Leave to marinate for 1 hour, turning once. Cook on barbecue, turning as needed and basting often with the cider-honey mixture, until cooked through and well glazed. (See chart, page 22.) Serve with any remaining baste as a sauce if you wish.

Bacon Chops in Ale

England

INGREDIENTS	Imperial	Metric	American
Bacon chops (green bacon)	6	6	6
Beer	1/2 pt.	300 ml.	1 1/4 cups
Freshly ground black pepper			
Bay leaf	1	1	1
Onions, sliced	3	3	3
Black treacle (molasses)	2 fl. oz.	60 ml.	1/4 cup
Juice of 1/2 lemon			
Oil for frying			

Put the bacon chops in a shallow dish. Add the beer, pepper, bay leaf and sliced onion. Cover and refrigerate overnight. Strain off the beer marinade into a saucepan. Start the bacon chops cooking on the barbecue (or under the grill). Boil the beer marinade until reduced by half, then add the treacle (molasses) and lemon juice. Brush the marinade over the chops as a baste, turn them and re-baste. Continue cooking until tender and glazed (see chart, page 22). Put the remaining onions in a stout frying pan, sprinkle with oil and fry on the barbecue grill until soft. Cover the chops with them and with any remaining marinade.

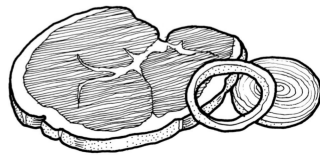

KEBABS, KOFTAS AND SO ON

Russia, Greece, Turkey and Iran all claim to have invented the idea of cooking portions of meat on skewers long ago. All we know is that kebab cookery appears to go back about 8,000 years in Greece and Turkey.

It is probably just as old in other parts of the world, and for the same reason. The quickest, and often the only way, in which herdsmen or warriors, guerrillas or bandits could cook themselves a hot meal in a hurry was to spear the meat they killed on an arrow, sword or pointed bone, and grill it over a camp-fire – in other words a barbecue.

Today each country, and even each region, prepares its meat differently, and is proud of its own version. You'll find some of the recipes below, so you can try them out on your own barbecue.

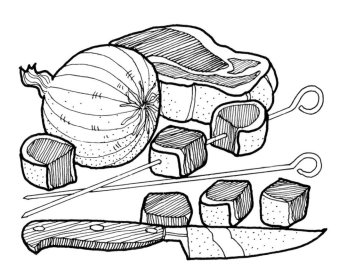

Shaslik (Russian Kebabs)

Russia

INGREDIENTS	Imperial	Metric	American
Leg of lamb	3½ lb.	1.6 kg.	3½ lb.
Salt and pepper			
Onions, skinned	12 oz.	340 g.	12 oz.
Juice of 3 large lemons			
Butter or oil			
Optional			
Tomatoes	1 lb.	450 g.	1 lb.
Bacon	8 oz.	225 g.	8 oz.
Green peppers, cored and de-seeded	12 oz.	340 g.	12 oz.

Remove any fat and bones from the meat. Cut it into pieces, about 2 in/5 cm square and ½ in/1 cm thick. Slice the onions thickly. Squeeze the lemon juice. Layer the meat and onions in a glass or earthenware bowl or crock, pour the lemon juice over and leave overnight.

Shortly before cooking, if you use the optional ingredients, quarter or slice the tomatoes thickly, and cut the bacon and pepper flesh into squares. Drain the meat. Thread meat, onions, tomatoes, bacon and peppers alternately on long skewers. Brush with fat or oil. Cook on the barbecue, turning often, for 20–30 minutes or until well cooked through (see chart, page 22).

Serves 6–8.

Russians would serve the shaslik as a main picnic course with a smoked fish pâté or dip such as Smoked Mackerel Dip (page 32) and Spicy Mushrooms (page 33) first and a fruit tart or gâteau afterwards. Breads, sausages, potato salad and pickled fruit would be eaten with the shaslik.

Cidered Sausage Skuets

England

INGREDIENTS	Imperial	Metric	American
For the cider baste			
Medium dry cider	*6 tbsp.*	*6 tbsp.*	*6 tbsp.*
Clear honey	*6 tbsp.*	*6 tbsp.*	*6 tbsp.*
Tomato paste	*3 tbsp.*	*3 tbsp.*	*3 tbsp.*
Juice of 1 lemon			
Large English pork sausages (2 oz./50 g. each)	*3 lb.*	*1.5 kg.*	*3 lb.*
Thin streaky bacon rashers without rind	*12*	*12*	*12*
Small button mushrooms	*8 oz.*	*225 g.*	*1/2 lb.*
Oil			
Salt and pepper			

Shortly ahead of time, stir the baste ingredients in a saucepan over medium heat until well blended.

Pinch the sausages in the middle, then twist them to make 2 short links of each. Separate the links. Wrap each in a bacon rasher. Thread the stubby sausages onto 12 kebab skewers alternately with the button mushrooms. Brush with oil and season lightly. Cook on the barbecue, turning often and brushing with the baste, until cooked through. If serving on plates, spoon a little extra baste over each skuet before serving.

Skuets were brought to England by the Normans.

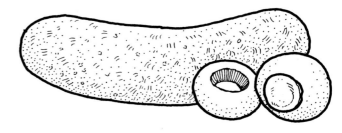

Cidered Sausage Skuets with Mardi Gras Sausages, page 55, and Chip-'n-Chutney Cheesy Spuds, page 65

Sasaties (Sweet Curried Skewered Lamb)

South Africa

INGREDIENTS	Imperial	Metric	American
Fat leg of lamb	3 lb.	1.5 kg.	3 lb.
Garlic clove	1/2	1/2	1/2
Large onions skinned	4	4	4
Light soft brown sugar	2 tbsp.	2 tbsp.	2 tbsp.
Milk	1/2 pt.	300 ml.	1 1/4 cups
Lamb dripping	1 tbsp.	1 tbsp.	1 tbsp.
Sweetened lime juice cordial (undiluted)	1 tbsp.	1 tbsp.	1 tbsp.
Curry powder	1 tbsp.	1 tbsp.	1 tbsp.
Whole cloves	1/2 tsp.	1/2 tsp.	1/2 tsp.
Whole allspice	1/2 tsp.	1/2 tsp.	1/2 tsp.
White wine vinegar	4 fl. oz.	120 ml.	1/2 cup
Salt and pepper			
Melted lamb dripping for brushing			
Flour	1 tbsp.	1 tbsp.	1 tbsp.
Chilled butter	1 tbsp.	1 tbsp.	1 tbsp.

Cut the lamb into 2 in/5 cm cubes, fat and lean together. Rub the inside of a large earthenware bowl with the cut side of the garlic clove. Lay the meat in the bowl. Slice 2 onions, add them to the meat with the sugar, and pour the milk over them. Slice the remaining 2 onions, and fry them in the dripping until lightly browned. Add the lime juice, whole spices, vinegar and seasoning. Pour the whole lot over the meat and leave overnight.

Remove the meat and onions with a slotted spoon. Thread them on 6 skewers, alternating meat and onions. Pat dry, and brush with melted dripping.

Before cooking the sasaties, turn the marinade into a saucepan. Sprinkle the flour over it. Bring to the boil, stirring constantly, and cook until slightly thickened. Stir in the chilled butter.

Cook the sasaties on the barbecue grill, turning several times, for about 20 minutes or until cooked through. Serve with Yellow Rice (page 66), fruit chutney and a green salad, and with the sauce in a jug.

Apart from steaks, sasaties are one of the most popular foods at a South African *braaivleis* (pronounced bryflace) which is the local name for a barbecue. Actually a real braaivleis isn't quite like a barbecue as we know it. A fairly deep trench is dug in an open space, and a layer of dry wood and charcoal is put in the bottom and lit. When this is smouldering well, more fuel is added, and this is repeated until the trench is 1/2–2/3rd full. Sturdy wire grids are then laid over the centre part of the trench to grill the food on.

Only raw steaks and chops and perhaps boerewors (sausages) and sasaties are cooked as a rule, and only chunks of bread with butter, green salad and fresh fruit are served with them, but there is always plenty of beer. In fact South Africans are even known to douse the barbecue flare-ups with beer. They say it makes the smoke smell wonderful.

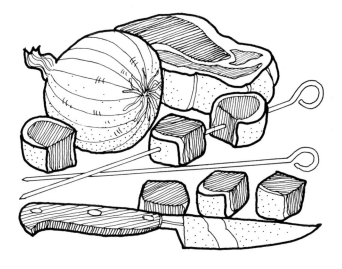

Chelow Kabab

Iran

INGREDIENTS	Imperial	Metric	American
Boneless mutton from leg or shoulder	*1½ lb.*	*750 g.*	*1½ lb.*
Salt	*1½ tsp.*	*1½ tsp.*	*1½ tsp.*
Pinch of pepper			
Natural yoghurt	*6 fl. oz.*	*175 ml.*	*¾ cup*
Oil for cooking			
Tomatoes, halved	*4*	*4*	*4*
Potato crisps			
Optional			
Long-grain rice	*12 oz.*	*340 g.*	*2 cups*
Salt			
Egg yolks	*4*	*4*	*4*
Butter	*2 oz.*	*50 g.*	*¼ cup*

Cut the mutton into strips about 7 × 2 in/17.5 × 5 cm in size. Rub salt and pepper into both sides well. Marinate them in yoghurt for 3 hours. While marinating, season the tomatoes and brush with oil.

Weave the meat strips lengthways onto long skewers. Beat them out flat with a mallet. Oil them lightly. Cook them on the barbecue, turning 2 or 3 times (see chart, page 22). Meanwhile, cook the tomatoes in a double-sided grill over the coals. Put the crisps in a biscuit tin with holes punched in it, and heat through on the coals. Serve all three items together.

Traditionally these kababs are served with rice boiled in salted water. The rice is put in individual bowls with an egg yolk and dab of butter in the centre of each bowl. The egg and butter are mashed into the hot rice and eaten with the meat. Instead of crisps, you could cook the rice ahead and keep it hot in a food flask if you are making the kababs as the single main dish for a small group.

Chelow Kabab and Grilled Kofta with Soudzoukakia (*left*) and sauce, page 58, and Sweet Barbecued Fruits, page 67

Grilled Kofta (Minced Meat Kebabs)

Turkey   Illustration far left

INGREDIENTS	Imperial	Metric	American
Day-old bread slices	*3*	*3*	*3*
White wine	*3 tbsp.*	*3 tbsp.*	*3 tbsp.*
Lamb from leg or shoulder, minced	*1 lb.*	*450 g.*	*1 lb.*
Medium onion, chopped	*1*	*1*	*1*
Egg (size 3)	*1*	*1*	*1*
Parsley sprigs, leaves only	*4*	*4*	*4*
Salt and black pepper			
Olive oil			

Cut the crusts off the bread and moisten it with the wine and a little water if needed. Squeeze it quite dry and put it with all the other ingredients except the olive oil in a food processor. Process until very smooth and pasty. With floured hands shape into rissoles the size of small eggs, and leave to stand on a cake rack for 30 minutes, then mould the kofta round flattened 'shish kebab' skewers (page 15). Brush with olive oil. Make sure the fire is hot. Cook, turning often, until well browned on all sides. (See chart, page 22.) Serve on bread with Two-Way Yoghurt Dressing 1 (page 72).

Every Middle Eastern country has its own types of kofta; Turkey alone has dozens of different ones. This is a fairly basic version. You could make beef ones using butcher's mince if it is easier to get than minced lamb. In this case use soft breadcrumbs instead of the day-old bread and wine, and add a little extra flavouring such as a pinch of ground coriander or chilli powder.

Mississippi Grill

U.S.A.

INGREDIENTS	Metric	Imperial	American
Pork fillet	1 lb.	450 g.	1 lb.
Eating apples	2	2	2
Pure corn oil	4 tbsp.	4 tbsp.	4 tbsp.
Green peppers, de-seeded	2	2	2
Button mushrooms	4 oz.	100 g.	4 oz.
Small tomatoes	6	6	6
Salt and pepper			

Cut the pork into 24 cubes. Core the apples and cut into slices about ½ in/1 cm thick; brush at once with the corn oil, reserving any oil left over. Cut the flesh of the peppers into squares. Thread pork cubes, apple slices, mushrooms, pepper squares and tomatoes on 6 skewers. Brush generously with the remaining oil. Cook on the barbecue, turning as needed until the pork is well cooked through (see chart, page 22).

Pop-Group Kebabs

New Zealand

INGREDIENTS	Imperial	Metric	American
For the marinade			
Oil	2 tbsp.	2 tbsp.	2 tbsp.
Red wine vinegar	1 tbsp.	1 tbsp.	1 tbsp.
Garlic clove, crushed	1	1	1
Onions cut in pieces	2	2	2
Salt and pepper			
For the kebabs			
Lamb from leg or shoulder	1 lb.	450 g.	1 lb.
Lambs' kidneys, skinned	4	4	4
Medium tomatoes	4	4	4
Green pepper, de-seeded	1	1	1
Button mushrooms	8–12	8–12	8–12
Fresh bay leaves	8	8	8
Salt and pepper			

Mix the ingredients for the marinade in a shallow dish, keeping a few pieces of onion aside for the kebabs. Cut the lamb into 1 in/2.5 cm cubes, and soak in the marinade for several hours or overnight, turning once or twice.

Cut the kidneys in half and core them. Quarter the tomatoes. Cut the pepper into pieces and blanch in boiling water for 3 minutes. Thread the lamb kidneys, tomatoes, pepper, mushrooms, bay leaves and reserved onion onto 4 long or 8 shorter kebab skewers. Season well. Cook on the barbecue, turning frequently, until done as you wish (see chart, page 22). Serve with Yellow Rice (page 66).

If you haven't time to marinate the meat, try this British version: Kidney Kebabs. You'll need 8 lamb's kidneys, halved, 4 bacon rashers cut in squares, 12 blanched baby onions, 3 quartered tomatoes and 12 button mushroom caps. Season the vegetables well with salt and pepper. Then thread all the items on 4 long skewers beginning and ending with kidney. Brush with oil or melted dripping, and grill. (Illustration page 36.)

A-Me'Huat (Beef Kebabs)

Burma

INGREDIENTS	Imperial	Metric	American
Good roasting beef	1 lb.	450 g.	1 lb.
Vinegar	1 tbsp.	1 tbsp.	1 tbsp.
Ground ginger	1 tbsp.	1 tbsp.	1 tbsp.
Turmeric	1/4 tsp.	1/4 tsp.	1/4 tsp.
Ground coriander	1 tsp.	1 tsp.	1 tsp.
Cumin seeds	1/4 tsp.	1/4 tsp.	1/4 tsp.
Soured milk	3 tbsp.	3 tbsp.	3 tbsp.
Salt	1 1/2 tsp.	1 1/2 tsp.	1 1/2 tsp.
Butter, melted	3 tbsp.	3 tbsp.	3 tbsp.

Cut the meat into 1 in/2.5 cm cubes. Put them in a bowl and sprinkle with the vinegar. Mix the spices together, add the soured milk and salt and pour the mixture over the beef. Leave to stand for 30 minutes. Thread 3 or 4 beef cubes on each of 8 small skewers. Brush with butter. Cook on the barbecue, turning 2–3 times. (See chart, page 22.) Baste with butter while cooking. Serve 2 small skewers to each person with Yellow Rice (page 66) and with Bean Sprout and Fruit Salad (page 68).

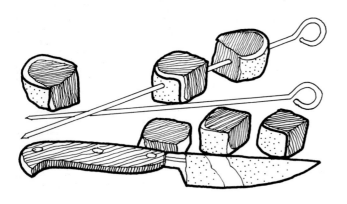

Shish Kebab

Turkey

INGREDIENTS	Imperial	Metric	American
For one marinade			
Olive oil	1/4 pt.	150 ml.	2/3 cup
Small onions pulped in a food processor	2	2	2
Fresh bay leaves, chopped	2	2	2
Dried oregano	2 tsp.	2 tsp.	2 tsp.
Juice of 1 lemon			
Salt and pepper			
For an alternative marinade			
Natural yoghurt	1/2 pt.	300 ml.	1 1/4 cups
Small onion pulped in a food processor	1	1	1
Salt and black pepper			
For the kebabs			
Leg of young lamb	2 lb.	1 kg.	2 lb.

Mix all the ingredients for the marinade you choose. Cut the meat into 1 in/2.5 cm cubes. Marinate it for 12 hours to make it really tender. Drain the cubes and thread them on shish kebab skewers. Make sure that the barbecue fire is very hot. Grill the skewers, turning often, for about 10 minutes, until the meat is dark brown outside but still juicy inside. It should be taken off the skewers and tipped into hollowed Pitta (page 72) or onto a 'bed' of hot rice.

The proper skewers for shish kebab are shaped like swords, broader at one end than the other and flattened to prevent the meat twisting on the skewer while cooking. Turkish skewers may be 8 ft/2.4 metres long. Obviously the pieces of meat have to be a lot larger for those!

Chicken Satay

Indonesia

INGREDIENTS	Imperial	Metric	American
For the marinade			
Salt	*1½ tsp.*	*1½ tsp.*	*1½ tsp.*
Freshly ground black pepper to taste			
Thick coconut milk (see below)	*4 fl. oz.*	*120 ml.*	*½ cup*
For the meat			
Medium (3 lb./1.5 kg.) chicken	*1*	*1*	*1*
For the sauce			
Smooth peanut butter	*4 tbsp.*	*4 tbsp.*	*4 tbsp.*
Chilli powder	*½ tsp.*	*½ tsp.*	*½ tsp.*
Lemon rind, grated	*1 tsp.*	*1 tsp.*	*1 tsp.*
Soft brown sugar	*1½ tsp.*	*1½ tsp.*	*1½ tsp.*
Water	*8 fl. oz.*	*225 ml.*	*1 cup*
Juice of ½ lime			

Mix the seasonings and coconut milk. Skin the chicken, cut the meat off the bones and cut it into 1½ in/3.5 cm pieces. Marinate the pieces in the coconut milk mixture for 1–2 hours. Drain, reserving the marinade. Thread 4 pieces of meat tightly on 6 short skewers. Put aside.

To make the sauce, mix all the ingredients except the lime juice in a saucepan. Simmer for 20 minutes. Take off the heat and stir in the juice. Put in a vacuum flask.

Cook the chicken on the barbecue, turning as needed, until tender. (See chart, page 22.) Baste with marinade often while cooking. Serve with the satay sauce and with Bean Sprout and Fruit Salad (page 68).

To make a fair substitute for coconut milk (obtained by grinding fresh coconut and squeezing it through a cloth), process 4 tbsp./60 ml. desiccated coconut in a blender adding 6 fl. oz./175 ml. hot water gradually, or use coconut cream sold in blocks at health food stores.

Chicken Satay with Pineapple Slaw, page 68, and Kalbi-Kui, page 40

SOME SPIT SPECIALITIES

Greek Meat on a Spit

Barbecuing is the most popular way of cooking in Greece, and a religious tradition as well. Greeks traditionally spit-roast a whole lamb or goat over a pit of burning charcoal for their Easter feast (which is more important in their Church than Christmas).

You probably won't want to spit-roast a whole lamb for a party at home but you may want to serve *souvlakia* which are the simplest form of kebab, and you will quite likely come across *doner kebab* (turning kebab) and *kokoretsi* which are only made by professional cooks in Greece.

Souvlakia may be tiny pieces of meat impaled on small splits of bamboo and served before meals with wine, or they can be main-meal kebabs, made from leg of lamb cut into 1 in/2.5 cm cubes, barbecued over charcoal and served with thick chunks of Greek bread. They are always marinated in olive oil and lemon juice with fresh chopped oregano and seasonings for some hours first, and are served with parsley and lemon. Large souvlakia are often grilled with bay leaves between the chunks of meat, or thick slices of tomato or onion.

Doner kebab in Greece consist of lamb cut from the rump, highly seasoned with garlic and herbs, and wound round a vertical skewer, in a shape like a huge carrot. The charcoal fire is open at the side facing the skewer which revolves slowly all the time, so that the outside of the 'carrot' steadily gets cooked. The cook carves off thin slices vertically with a sharp knife, and as the shaved meat falls into a tin pan below, the still uncooked inner part of the 'carrot' is exposed – to get cooked in its turn. Doner kebab meat is served with sliced onion, chopped parsley and a sprinkling of cayenne.

Kokoretsi are sausages (almost!) made of the highly seasoned lamb variety meats, the heart, liver, kidneys and sweetbreads. The meats are coarsely chopped and moulded into a sausage shape with the intestines wound round it. It is then skewered or spitted and charcoal-grilled slowly for several hours, being basted with the inevitable Middle Eastern olive oil and lemon juice. It is not an aristocratic dish but it can be very good.

In England, a whole lamb is roasted at the Whit Monday Ram Roasting Fair in Devon, and roasting a whole hog, sheep or even an ox is becoming a popular 'draw' at charity functions. Usually a professional roasting chef or butcher is called in to supervise the cooking and to carve the meat.

Spitted Turkish Lamb

The marinades for shish kebab (page 50) are also used for a whole leg of young lamb before spit-roasting it. Have the meat boned and tied or rolled; it will be easier to balance it on the spit (see page 24). Pierce it in several places with a knife-point, then marinate it for 2–4 hours. Make sure the fire is very hot, and, for extra scent, add herbs (page 29) to the coals. Spit-roast for 30 minutes per pound, brushing the meat with marinade from time to time. After about 40 minutes, you can start carving off the outer slices of the meat as it roasts in the same way as a doner kebab is cut. Serve it in the same way.

All over the Middle East, a leg or whole lamb is spit-roasted for any feast or solemn religious occasion if the family concerned can afford it.

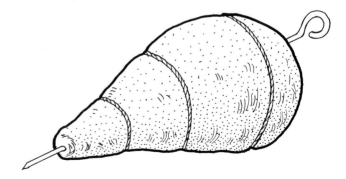

Chicken on a Spit (à la Broche)

France

INGREDIENTS	Imperial	Metric	American
3 lb./1.5 kg. chicken with neck skin left on	1	1	1
Salt and pepper			
Chicken liver	1	1	1
Tarragon sprigs, fresh or dried	2	2	2
Butter	6 tbsp.	6 tbsp.	6 tbsp.
Water	3 tbsp.	3 tbsp.	3 tbsp.

Wipe the bird dry inside and out; do not wash it. Season it inside. Season the bird's liver and put it in the bird with a sprig of tarragon and 2 tablespoons of the butter. Turn back the neck skin over the breast to prevent the breast drying out. Truss the limbs in the same place on each side so that the bird will be evenly balanced on the spit (page 24).

Spit the chicken lengthways, and put it over the fire. Put a small drip tray under it containing the remaining tarragon sprig, 2 more tbsp. butter and the water. Spit-roast for about 45 minutes until the skin is golden-brown and bubbled. While carving the bird, add the remaining butter to the juices in the drip tray and heat, stirring, over the hottest part of the fire to make a sauce if needed.

Serves 4–6.

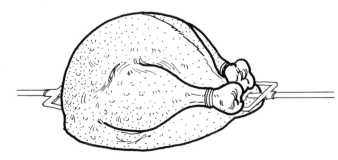

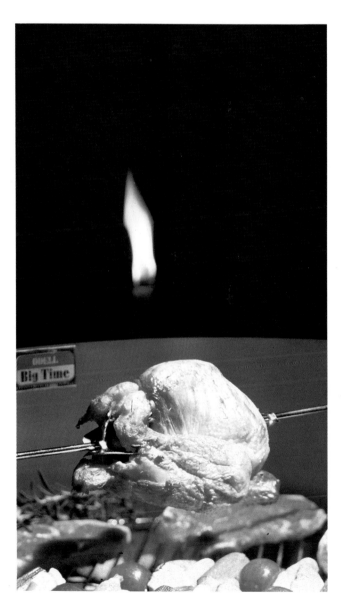

Barbecued Bangers with Husked Indian Corn, page 66

SAUSAGES AND BURGERS

Barbecued Bangers
England

INGREDIENTS	Imperial	Metric	American
For the sauce			
Canned peeled tomatoes	8 oz.	227 g.	½ lb.
Dry still cider	2½ fl. oz.	75 ml.	⅓ cup
Tomato ketchup (catsup)	1½ fl. oz.	40 ml.	3 tbsp.
Worcestershire sauce	4 tsp.	4 tsp.	5 tsp.
Bay leaves (small)	2	2	2
Garlic clove, finely chopped	1	1	1
Onion, chopped	3 tbsp.	3 tbsp.	3 tbsp.
Celery stalks, finely chopped	2–3	2–3	2–3
Lemon, thin slices	4	4	4
Muscovado sugar	4 tsp.	4 tsp.	5 tsp.
Water	½ pt.	300 ml.	1¼ cups
For the grill			
Onion, peeled	4	4	4
Large English pork sausages	2 lb.	1 kg.	2 lb.

Put all the barbecue sauce ingredients in a saucepan. Cover and simmer for 30 minutes. Adjust seasoning. Pour into a vacuum flask and stopper securely until needed. Cut the onions for grilling into wedges. Thread the sausages lengthways on long skewers with the onion wedges between them. Cook on the barbecue, turning with tongs, until golden-brown on all sides. Pour the sauce into a bowl and use as a dip.

Savoury Burgers

International   Illustration page 37

INGREDIENTS	Imperial	Metric	American
For the burgers			
Good quality minced beef	1 lb.	450 g.	1 lb.
Small onion, finely chopped	1	1	1
Salt and pepper			
For the barbecue relish			
Butter	2 oz.	50 g.	¼ cup
Medium onion, chopped	1	1	1
Canned tomatoes, drained	13½ oz.	396 g.	13½ oz.
Apricot chutney (sweet pickle)	4 tbsp.	4 tbsp.	4 tbsp.
Dried marjoram	¼ tsp.	¼ tsp.	¼ tsp.
Salt and pepper			
For the savoury butter			
Butter, softened	4 oz.	100 g.	½ cup
Horseradish sauce	1½ tbsp.	1½ tbsp.	1½ tbsp.
Dijon or Meaux mustard	1 tbsp.	1 tbsp.	1 tbsp.
Black peppercorns, coarsely ground	1 tbsp.	1 tbsp.	1 tbsp.

Mix together the beef and onion. Season well. Shape into 4 patties about 3 in/7.5 cm across. Stack with clingfilm between each, cover and chill until ready to use. Make the relish: fry the onion gently in the butter in a medium saucepan until soft but not browned. Add the remaining ingredients, seasoning to taste. Cook gently until thick (about 20 minutes). Sieve, then leave to cool. Make the savoury butter by mixing all the ingredients together thoroughly.

Brush the burgers well with the relish on both sides. Cook on the barbecue for 5–7 minutes on each side, basting frequently with savoury butter. Put a dab of cold relish on each before serving in baps or Burger Buns (page 73), wrapped in foil and warmed on the hot coals.

You can vary this basic recipe in a lot of ways. For other meat burgers, try a mixture of minced lamb, beef and bacon or of fresh pork and sausagemeat. Add a little grated carrot, crushed garlic, chopped mushrooms, fresh breadcrumbs, or a dash or two of ketchup, Worcestershire sauce or soy sauce. Alternatively make the savoury butter with a herb-flavoured mustard such as chive or horseradish, or with anchovy sauce or essence. Substitute Piquant Butter (page 37) for the Savoury Butter if you wish, and spread the cut buns with the butter before filling.

Mardi Gras Sausages

England   Illustration page 44

INGREDIENTS	Imperial	Metric	American
English-style pancakes	8	8	8
Medium onions, sliced in rings	4	4	4
Oil for frying			
Large English beef sausages (2 oz./50 g.) each	1 lb.	450 g.	1 lb.
Sweetcorn relish			

Shortly before barbecuing, reheat made-ahead pancakes in a foil-wrapped stack in the oven. Transfer to an insulated bag with heated cold packs, or place over a candle-warmer on your barbecue serving table. Fry onion rings in oil until crisp and keep warm with the pancakes.

At barbecue time, cook the sausages on the barbecue until cooked through and well browned. Stack the sausages on the serving table with the pancakes, open pot of relish and onion rings. Spread a spoonful of relish on each pancake, place a sausage on top and roll the pancake around it. Garnish with onion rings. Serve on cardboard plates with forks.

Lamburgers

New Zealand

INGREDIENTS	Imperial	Metric	American
Onion, finely chopped	1	1	1
Pure corn oil	2 tbsp.	2 tbsp.	2 tbsp.
Boneless lamb shoulder minced (ground)	1 lb.	450 g.	1 lb.
Celery stalk, finely chopped	1	1	1
Tomato purée	1 tbsp.	1 tbsp.	1 tbsp.
Tomato ketchup (catsup)	1 tbsp.	1 tbsp.	1 tbsp.
Dried mixed herbs	1 tsp.	1 tsp.	1 tsp.
Soft white breadcrumbs	2 oz.	50 g.	½ cup
For the Barbecue Sauce			
Small onion, finely chopped	1	1	1
Celery stalk, finely chopped	1	1	1
Garlic clove, crushed	1	1	1
Pure corn oil	2 tbsp.	2 tbsp.	2 tbsp.
Dry mustard	2 tbsp.	2 tbsp.	2 tbsp.
Demerara sugar	2 tbsp.	2 tbsp.	2 tbsp.
Tabasco	½ tsp.	½ tsp.	½ tsp.
Tomato juice	12 fl. oz.	350 ml.	1½ cups
Worcestershire sauce	2 tbsp.	2 tbsp.	2 tbsp.
Juice of 1 grapefruit			
Red wine vinegar	4 tbsp.	4 tbsp.	4 tbsp.
Bay leaf	1	1	1

Fry the onion gently in the oil until soft. Mix the onions and oil with all the other ingredients, seasoning to taste. Shape into 8 patties about 1 in/2.5 cm thick. Cook them on the barbecue for 5–7 minutes on each side, depending on how well done you want them.

You could make these burgers with braising meat from a ½ carcass or other large pack of assorted freezer cuts, and team it with lamb chops (see chart, page 22) and with Pop-Group Kebabs (page 49) as a complete freezer meal. Serve it with the Barbecue Sauce and with a rice salad or slaw including fresh chopped pineapple and walnuts.

For the sauce
In a medium-sized saucepan, fry the onion, celery and garlic in the oil until soft but not brown. Add the remaining ingredients, bring to the boil, then simmer for 10 minutes.

Hey Presto Burgers

England

INGREDIENTS	Imperial	Metric	American
Onions, sliced	3	3	3
Butter	2 oz.	50 g.	¼ cup
Turkey burgers	6	6	6
Butter for brushing			
Baps or home-made Burger			
Buns (page 73)	6	6	6
Cheddar cheese, diced			
(optional)	2 oz.	50 g.	¼ cup
Sliced tomatoes			
Gherkins			
Watercress			

Fry the sliced onions in the butter until lightly browned. Cook the burgers on the barbecue for 5–7 minutes on each side or a little longer if still frozen. Baste with butter while cooking (use the butter from cooking the onions if there is some). Split the buns, and brush a little butter over the cut sides. Lay a burger on the bottom half of each and top with onion rings and a few cubes of cheese if used. Serve with sliced tomato, gherkins and watercress from your barbecue serving table.

Store-bought burgers are a useful backstop since you can keep them frozen until the moment you need them. Try doubling them for man-sized helpings, putting the onion rings and cheese between 2 burgers.

Soudzoukakia (Sausages)

Greece   Illustration page 46

INGREDIENTS	Imperial	Metric	American
Soft white breadcrumbs	4 oz.	100 g.	4 oz.
Milk	1/4 pt.	150 ml.	2/3 cup
Minced meat (any kind or mixed)	2 lb.	1 kg.	2 lb.
Onion, grated	2 tbsp.	2 tbsp.	2 tbsp.
Garlic cloves, finely chopped	3	3	3
Salt and pepper			
Flour			
Olive oil			
For the sauce			
Canned or very ripe skinned tomatoes (3 × 13½ oz./396 g. cans)	2 lb.	1 kg.	2 lb.
Sugar	2 tsp.	2 tsp.	2 tsp.
Bay leaves	2	2	2
Pinch of ground cumin			
Small onion	1	1	1
Salt to taste			

Moisten the breadcrumbs with the milk. Squeeze dry. Mix with the meat, grated onion and chopped garlic and season well. Shape into fat little sausages about 2 in/5 cm long. Roll in flour. Brush with oil and cook on the barbecue or fry. Put all the sauce ingredients in a pan, leaving the onion whole, and simmer the sauce for 45 minutes. Remove the onion and bay leaves and sieve the rest. Reheat if needed. Keep hot in a food flask and use as a dip; or if serving indoors at the table, simmer the sausages in the sauce for the last 15 minutes.

Makes about 32 sausages.

Greek Sausages or Keftethes

Greece

INGREDIENTS	Imperial	Metric	American
Medium onion, finely chopped	1	1	1
Fresh breadcrumbs	2 oz.	50 g.	1/2 cup
Milk			
Beef mince	12 oz.	340 g.	12 oz.
Beaten egg	1	1	1
Parsley, chopped	1 tbsp.	1 tbsp.	1 tbsp.
Mint, finely chopped	1/2 tsp.	1/2 tsp.	1/2 tsp.
Hard cheese, finely grated	1 tbsp.	1 tbsp.	1 tbsp.
Flour	1 oz.	25 g.	1/4 cup
Salt and pepper			
Flour for dusting			
Oil			

Put the onion in a strainer, and pour boiling water over it. Sprinkle the breadcrumbs with a little milk. Process the meat in a food processor or blender until pasty. Add all the other ingredients except the flour for dusting and the oil, and process to a paste. With floured hands, shape the paste into 12–14 balls a little larger than golf-balls. Then roll them between your palms to the same shape and length as chipolata sausages. Roll in flour. Brush with oil and cook on the barbecue in a double-sided grill, turning as needed, until cooked through and well browned.

Keftethes are made in the same way but you just squeeze the balls of mixture slightly to make them into ovals like stubby fat sausages. They are generally deep-fried, but they can be cooked on the barbecue like the thinner sausages. In Greece, both are eaten as snacks with wine while waiting for the Greek Easter Lamb to cook over its bed of coals (page 52).

Vealburgers

France

INGREDIENTS	Imperial	Metric	American
Garlic clove, peeled	*1*	*1*	*1*
Canned ratatouille	*¼ pt.*	*150 ml.*	*⅔ cup*
Salt			
Dried basil or thyme	*½ tsp.*	*½ tsp.*	*½ tsp.*
Cooked white rice	*2 oz.*	*50 g.*	*⅓ cup*
Lean raw veal	*1 lb.*	*450 g.*	*1 lb.*
Boiled gammon, ham or			
* bacon*	*2 oz.*	*50 g.*	*¼ cup*
Chopped parsley	*2 tbsp.*	*2 tbsp.*	*2 tbsp.*
Pepper	*¼ tsp.*	*¼ tsp.*	*¼ tsp.*
Egg, beaten			
Flour			
Melted butter and oil,			
* mixed*			

Squeeze the garlic over the ratatouille and season with a little salt if needed. Add the herb. Simmer for 5 minutes or until any free liquid with the ratatouille has almost evaporated. Mince the rice and both meats together finely. Add to the ratatouille with the parsley. Mix well. Taste and season with salt and pepper. Mix in enough egg (about 1 tbsp.) to bind the ingredients. With floured hands, shape the mixture into 8 burgers about ½ in/1 cm thick (2 oz./ 50 g. each). Refrigerate until needed. Just before cooking, dredge the burgers with the flour and brush with mixed butter and oil. Cook on the barbecue, turning once, for 6–7 minutes on each side. Baste with butter and oil from time to time while cooking.

Serve with Barbecue Sauce (page 56) if liked.

POULTRY

Marinated Chicken

U.S.A.

INGREDIENTS	Imperial	Metric	American
For the marinade			
Lemon juice	*2 tbsp.*	*2 tbsp.*	*2 tbsp.*
Oil	*3 tbsp.*	*3 tbsp.*	*3 tbsp.*
Worcestershire sauce	*1 tbsp.*	*1 tbsp.*	*1 tbsp.*
Garlic clove, crushed	*1*	*1*	*1*
Tomato ketchup (catsup)	*2 tbsp.*	*2 tbsp.*	*2 tbsp.*
Freshly ground black pepper			
Tabasco to taste			
For the chicken			
Chicken quarters	*4*	*4*	*4*
Seasoned flour			
Oil	*2 tbsp.*	*2 tbsp.*	*2 tbsp.*

Mix together all the marinade ingredients. Put in a large plastic bag. Prick the chicken quarters all over with a knife point, and add them to the bag. Close it securely, and refrigerate for several hours or overnight, turning 2 or 3 times.

Take the chicken out of the marinade, and roll in seasoned flour. Sprinkle with oil. Cook on the barbecue, turning often for 40 minutes or until golden and tender. Brush with marinade during cooking if you wish.

Jacket potatoes, topped with cheese and a small piece of preserved ginger, are a delicious addition to this spicy way of serving chicken.

Turkey Drummers

England   Illustration right

INGREDIENTS	Imperial	Metric	American
Turkey drumsticks, thawed if frozen			
For each drumstick			
Garlic clove, peeled and slivered lengthways	¼	¼	¼
Streaky bacon rashers, without rind	2–3	2–3	2–3
Oil for brushing			
Devilling Sauce (optional)			
For each drumstick			
Apricot jam	2 tbsp.	2 tbsp.	2 tbsp.
Tomato ketchup (catsup)	4 tbsp.	4 tbsp.	4 tbsp.
Soy sauce	1 tbsp.	1 tbsp.	1 tbsp.
French mustard	2 tsp.	2 tsp.	2 tsp.
Worcestershire sauce	1 tbsp.	1 tbsp.	1 tbsp.
Lemon juice	1 tbsp.	1 tbsp.	1 tbsp.
Salt and pepper			

Stick a garlic sliver in the thick end of each drumstick. Wrap the drumstick in bacon. Brush lightly with oil, and cook on the barbecue, turning often, until cooked through and tender. This will take about 2 hours. If you use a meat thermometer, cook until the temperature is 185°F/85°C.

If you prefer, cook the bacon separately, and brush the drumsticks while cooking with Devilling Sauce. To make it, melt the apricot jam with the ketchup in a heavy saucepan. Add all the other ingredients, and stir round. Bring to the boil, and cook for 1 minute. Oil and cook the drumsticks, brushing generously with sauce.

Honeyed Chicken Drumsticks

West Indies   Illustration page 64

INGREDIENTS	Imperial	Metric	American
Chicken drumsticks	10	10	10
Clear honey	4 tbsp.	4 tbsp.	4 tbsp.
Juice of 1 lemon			
Salt and pepper			
Natural demerara sugar	6 tbsp.	6 tbsp.	6 tbsp.

Prick the chicken all over with a skewer. Heat the honey and lemon juice together and brush it over the drumsticks. Season with salt and pepper, then roll each drumstick in demerara sugar. Cook on the barbecue, turning often, until golden and tender (see chart, page 22). The sugar will make a crunchy coating. Wrap a foil frill around the bone end of each drumstick for easy eating. Serve with Bacon-Wrapped Corn (page 64) and foil-wrapped jacket potatoes filled with soured cream.

FISH

See also page 64–65 in the section on Foil-Cooked Food.

Sweet-Sour Fish Kebabs

South-East Asia

INGREDIENTS	Imperial	Metric	American
For the marinade and baste			
Clear honey	4 tbsp.	4 tbsp.	4 tbsp.
Lemon juice	7 tsp.	7 tsp.	7 tsp.
Soy sauce	1 tbsp.	1 tbsp.	1 tbsp.
Pinch of chilli powder			
For the kebabs			
Medium-sized whiting or smallish red mullet about 14 oz./400 g. each	3	3	3
Medium-size onions, skinned	2	2	2
Medium-sized courgettes	4	4	4
Lemon	1	1	1

Warm all the marinade ingredients in a saucepan, stirring well. Keep warm.

Clean the fish and cut off the heads, fins and tails. Scale mullet. Wash the fish inside and out, and pat dry. Cut them across into 1½ in/3.5 cm slices, still with the skin on. Cut the onions into thin rings, and the courgettes into 1 in/2.5 cm slices, discarding the ends. Slice the lemon thinly. Thread the fish, vegetables and lemon slices alternately on 4 skewers. Lay them in a shallow dish and pour the marinade over them. Leave them for 30 minutes, turning them once or twice.

Take the skewers out of the marinade and shake off any free drips of marinade. Cook on the barbecue, basting with marinade and turning often for 12–15 minutes. Serve with Yellow Rice (page 66).

Split Herrings

England

INGREDIENTS	Imperial	Metric	American
Fresh herrings, about			
8 oz./225 g. each	6	6	6
For each herring			
Sprinkling of onion salt			
or powder			
Grinding of black pepper			
A few grains of cayenne			
Sprinkling of cider vinegar			
Melted butter for basting			

Clean the fish, cut off the heads, wash inside and out, and pat dry. Split the fish down the back, and bat out flat like kippers. Remove any visible bones. Sprinkle the fish with all the seasonings. Cook in a double-sided hinged grill, basting with butter and turning as needed until cooked through (5–7 minutes). Serve with lemon wedges.

Scottish Mackerel

Scotland

INGREDIENTS	Imperial	Metric	American
Medium mackerel,			
¾ lb.–1 lb./340–450 g.			
each			
For each mackerel			
Fine-cut marmalade	2 tbsp.	2 tbsp.	2 tbsp.
Salt and pepper			
Fine oatmeal	2 tsp.	2 tsp.	2 tsp.
Butter			
Chopped parsley			

Clean the fish, wash inside and out and pat dry. Cut 3 diagonal slits in the skin on each side. Smear the marmalade over the inside of the cavity. Skewer the opening to close. Season the fish on both sides and dust with oatmeal. Cook in a double-sided hinged grill over hot coals (see chart, page 23); turn and baste with butter often while cooking. Sprinkle with chopped parsley.

Bacon-Wrapped Corn with Honeyed Chicken Drumsticks,
page 61

FOIL-COOKED FOOD

Bacon-Wrapped Corn
U.S.A.

INGREDIENTS	Imperial	Metric	American
Corn on the cob	8	8	8
Middle cut bacon rashers			
without rind	8	8	8
Salt and pepper			
Butter	8 tbsp.	8 tbsp.	8 tbsp.

Remove the husks and silk of the corn if needed. Wrap each cob in a bacon rasher, and place it on a square of diamond foil. Sprinkle it with seasoning and top it with 1 tbsp./15 ml. butter. Fold the foil round it to make a parcel. Cook on the barbecue for 45 minutes, turning often. Unfold the foil for serving.

Double-Covered Onions
Europe   Illustration page 36

INGREDIENTS	Imperial	Metric	American
Large onions,			
12–14 oz./340–400 g.			
each			
For each onion			
Butter for greasing			
Salt			
Grated cheese or soured			
cream or Two-Way			
Yoghurt Dressing			
(page 72)	1 tbsp.	1 tbsp.	1 tbsp.

Cut out squares of foil which will each enclose an onion completely. Grease them well. Cut off the roots of the onions but do not skin them. Cut a deep cross in the top of each onion, almost down to the centre. Place one onion in the middle of each foil square and draw the foil up, twisting the edges into a knot over the top of the onion. Bake the onions in the oven at 350°F/180°C/Gas Mark 4 for about 1 hour until nearly cooked. Transfer to the barbecue and complete the cooking in the hot coals at the edge of the fire. Place each onion on a plate, open the foil, and fold back the brown skin. Open out the cut onion flesh a little with a spoon, then cover with the chosen topping and eat with a fork.

Florida Fish Fillets

U.S.A.

INGREDIENTS	Imperial	Metric	American
White fish fillets, skinned (cod, haddock, mullet, etc) 4–5 oz./100–150 g. each			
For each fillet			
Butter for greasing			
Salt	1 tsp.	1 tsp.	1 tsp.
Finely grated orange rind	1 tsp.	1 tsp.	1 tsp.
Finely grated grapefruit rind	1/2 tsp.	1/2 tsp.	1/2 tsp.
A few grains grated nutmeg			

Grease squares of foil big enough to enclose the fillets. Lay a fillet in the centre of each square. Sprinkle it with salt and rind. Fold the foil over the fish, allowing a good overlap. Fold over the ends in the same way. Cook the fish on the grill over hot coals for 25–30 minutes. Put the fish parcel on a plate, then open the foil and eat with a fork.

Chip-'N-Chutney Cheesy Spuds

England   Illustration page 44

INGREDIENTS	Imperial	Metric	American
For the filling			
Thick coating white sauce	1/2 pt.	300 ml.	1 1/4 cups
Grated cheese	6 oz.	175 g.	3/4 cup firmly packed
Salt and pepper			
Mild chutney	4 tbsp.	4 tbsp.	4 tbsp.
Chipolata sausages, cooked and chopped	1 lb.	450 g.	1 lb.
For the spuds			
Equal-sized large baking potatoes	12	12	12
Oil for brushing			

Heat the filling ingredients gently in a saucepan, then turn into a vacuum flask and seal. Brush the potatoes with oil, wrap in foil. Bake them for 2 hours in the glowing ash at the edge of a camp-fire or among the coals at the edge of a big barbecue. Alternatively, bake them in the oven before barbecuing and transfer to the barbecue when the fire is established to complete the cooking. Open the foil just enough to let you slit the potatoes open; pile chip-'n-chutney cheese mixture into each. Serve with spoons.

A super backstop dish to have ready to cope with extra-hearty appetites or numbers – or in case the rain comes down.

VEGETABLES AND FRUIT

Yellow Rice

South Africa   Illustration page 49

INGREDIENTS	Imperial	Metric	American
Water	*1¼ pts.*	*650 ml.*	*3 cups*
Long-grain rice	*7 oz.*	*200 g.*	*1 cup*
Cinnamon stick	*1*	*1*	*1*
Turmeric	*½ tsp.*	*½ tsp.*	*½ tsp.*
Salt	*1 tsp.*	*1 tsp.*	*1 tsp.*
Butter	*1 tbsp.*	*1 tbsp.*	*1 tbsp.*
Seedless raisins (optional)	*3 oz.*	*75 g.*	*½ cup*

Bring the water to the boil in a large saucepan over low heat. Sprinkle in the rice. Add all the other ingredients, and stir round once. Then cook until the rice is tender and all the water is absorbed. Add a little more water if the rice begins to dry out, but do not let it be soggy. Serve the rice hot with roasts, grills or barbecued dishes, or cool and use as a rice salad.

Husked Indian Corn

U.S.A.   Illustration page 54

INGREDIENTS	Imperial	Metric	American
Corn on the cob, in the husk	*1 per person*	*1 per person*	*1 per person*
Softened butter	*1 tbsp. per cob*	*1 tbsp. per cob*	*1 tbsp. per cob*

Strip back the husk of each corn cob without detaching it. Pull out the silky 'hair'. Spread the cob with softened butter. Re-fold the husk leaves over the cob. Thread each cob on a separate skewer or stick a small poultry skewer in each end of the cob. Cook on the barbecue, turning often with tongs. When the husks char, remove them and cook the cobs until the kernels begin to bronze. Serve on the skewers.

American corn is sold when younger than English corn. If the raw kernels do not dent easily and give out a milky liquid when pressed with a thumbnail, prepare them without butter, then parboil them before roasting. Cool, spread with butter and cook as above. Alternatively bake them in foil (page 64).

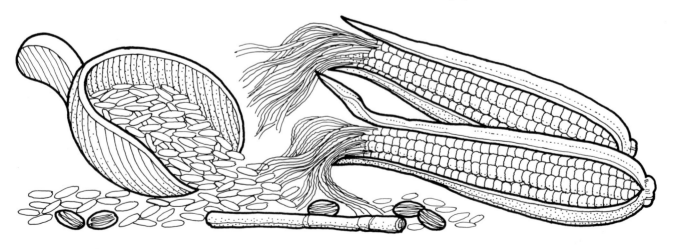

Mushroom Kebabs

Australia

INGREDIENTS	Imperial	Metric	American
Large button mushrooms	*16*	*16*	*16*
Small sweet red			
* peppers*	*2*	*2*	*2*
Large courgette	*1*	*1*	*1*
Medium-size firm			
* yellow banana*	*1*	*1*	*1*
Salt and pepper			
Melted butter			

Remove the mushroom stems. Core and de-seed the peppers, then cut the flesh of each pepper into 6 square pieces. Top and tail the courgette, cut the ends off the banana and cut each across into 12 slices. Thread the mushrooms, pepper squares, courgette and banana slices onto 4 skewers, beginning and ending with a mushroom. Season on all sides and brush with melted butter. Cook near the edge of the barbecue, turning often, until the pepper and courgette are tender.

Savoury and Sweet Barbecued Fruits

Illustration page 46

These fruits are especially popular in Australia. They are designed to be eaten with a spoon.

Bananas

Bury slightly underripe bananas in the hot coals and leave for 10 minutes or until the skin is just charred. Holding a banana in a piece of foil, peel off a strip of skin (with pliers or a piece of foil to grip with). Season with salt and pepper and serve with small spoons.

Apples

Core cooking apples without peeling them but split the skin around the middle like baked apples. Stuff with cooked savoury rice or with dried fruit. Top with a little butter. Wrap in foil like dumplings with the loose edges of foil twisted together at the top. Bury them in the coals for 1 hour. Unfold the foil at the top and serve with spoons.

Tomatoes

Cut a thin slice off the tops of tomatoes. Top them with a little chutney and dabs of soured cream. Wrap them in foil like apples. Cook beside the fire, turning the fruit round once or twice for about 30 minutes. Unfold the foil at the top and serve with spoons.

Sweet barbecued fruits

For sweet barbecued fruits you can thread apple, pear and tangerine slices, and pineapple cubes on skewers, sprinkle them with melted butter and natural light muscovado sugar. Grill them, turning often, until brown. Alternate pieces of each fruit on a skewer to make a delicious, colourful dessert.

SERVING TABLE SPECIALS – SALADS – DRESSINGS – BREAD AND ROLLS

A surprising number of salads can be made ahead of time; breads and rolls can be made and frozen days or even weeks ahead.

Pineapple Slaw

Australia   Illustration page 51

INGREDIENTS	Imperial	Metric	American
Firm white cabbage	*1¼ lb.*	*650 g.*	*1¼ lb.*
Small fresh pineapple			
about 2 lb./1 kg.	*1*	*1*	*1*
Walnut halves	*3 oz.*	*75 g.*	*½ cup*
Sharp dessert apple	*1*	*1*	*1*
For the dressing			
Mayonnaise	*2 fl. oz.*	*50 ml.*	*¼ cup*
Natural yoghurt	*4 fl. oz.*	*100 ml.*	*½ cup*
Salt and pepper			
Clear honey	*2 tsp.*	*2 tsp.*	*2 tsp.*
Lemon or orange juice			

Cut out the cabbage stalk and shred the leaves finely. Peel, quarter and core the pineapple, and cut the flesh into small cubes; add any free juice made while cutting it. Peel, quarter and core the apple. Cut the flesh into small cubes, and toss them at once with the pineapple juice and cubes. Mix both fruits and the juice with the cabbage. Reserve 6 or 8 walnut halves for garnishing the salad. Chop and mix in the rest.

Mix thoroughly the mayonnaise and yoghurt for the dressing, stirring until the yoghurt is liquid and smooth. Add a scrap of seasoning. Stir in the honey, then sharpen with 1 tsp./15 ml. juice or to taste, depending on the flavour of the yoghurt. Toss the slaw with the dressing, cover and refrigerate. Toss again and garnish just before serving.

Any slaw can be made ahead of time. This one is attractive because pineapple always goes well with grilled and barbecued foods. For a less sweet dressing, try the Creamy Mustard Mayonnaise on page 72.

Bean Sprout and Fruit Salad

Far East (European style)   Illustration page 69

INGREDIENTS	Imperial	Metric	American
Pasta shapes	*6 oz.*	*175 g.*	*6 oz.*
Salt			
7½ oz./210 g. can			
pineapple chunks	*1*	*1*	*1*
Bean sprouts	*6 oz.*	*175 g.*	*3 cups*
Carrots, shredded	*2*	*2*	*2*
Cucumber, sliced	*½*	*½*	*½*
For the dressing			
Pure corn oil	*4 fl. oz.*	*120 ml.*	*6 tbsp.*
Orange juice	*2 tbsp.*	*2 tbsp.*	*2 tbsp.*
Pineapple syrup from			
can	*2 tbsp.*	*2 tbsp.*	*2 tbsp.*
Soy sauce	*1 tbsp.*	*1 tbsp.*	*1 tbsp.*
Pinch of ground ginger			

Boil the pasta in salted water until just tender. Meanwhile drain the pineapple chunks, reserving the syrup. Mix 2 tbsp. pineapple syrup with the other dressing ingredients. Drain the pasta while still warm, and mix with the dressing. Cool well. Add the carrots, cucumber and pineapple chunks and toss; lastly add the bean sprouts. Mix in very lightly.

You could use long-grain rice instead of pasta for this salad to give it a more oriental character.

Serves 4.

Rainbow Salad

International

INGREDIENTS	Imperial	Metric	American
Carrots, grated	2	2	2
Button mushrooms,			
sliced	*4 oz.*	*100 g.*	*⅔ cup*
Cucumber, de-seeded and			
cut into			
'matchsticks'	*½*	*½*	*½*
Tomatoes, quartered	5	5	5
Celery stalks, sliced	4	4	4
Spring onions, chopped	2	2	2
Chopped chives	*1 tbsp.*	*1 tbsp.*	*1 tbsp.*
Chopped parsley	*1 tbsp.*	*1 tbsp.*	*1 tbsp.*
Onion rings			
For the dressing			
Olive oil	*8 tbsp.*	*8 tbsp.*	*8 tbsp.*
Lemon juice	*4 tbsp.*	*4 tbsp.*	*4 tbsp.*
Caster sugar	*½ tsp.*	*½ tsp.*	*½ tsp.*
Salt	*1 tsp.*	*1 tsp.*	*1 tsp.*
Freshly ground pepper			

Make the dressing first by mixing all the ingredients together. Toss the grated carrots in a bowl with 2 tbsp./ 30 ml. of the dressing. Arrange in a strip on a flat platter. Lay the mushrooms, cucumber, tomatoes and celery in strips alongside it. Sprinkle each with one of the garnishes, either chopped spring onion, chives, parsley or onion rings. Serve the rest of the dressing in a jug.

Serves 4.

This is another make-ahead salad. Cut up the vegetables and chill them in separate bowls the night before your barbecue. Assemble the salad early in the day and keep it covered with clingfilm in a cool place such as a larder until needed.

Bean Sprout and Fruit Salad, page 68

Danish Chef's Salad

Denmark

INGREDIENTS	Imperial	Metric	American
Cos lettuce	1/2	1/2	1/2
1 medium-sized bunch radishes			
Cucumber	2 in	5 cm	2 in
Onion	1	1	1
Cooked ham	8 oz.	225 g.	1/2 lb.
Danish Blue cheese	4 oz.	100 g.	2/3 cup
Salt and pepper			
Pinch of dry mustard			
Pinch of caster sugar			
Pure corn oil	4 tbsp.	4 tbsp.	4 tbsp.
White wine vinegar	2 tbsp.	2 tbsp.	2 tbsp.

Prepare and slice the lettuce and radishes, and slice the cucumber. Skin the onion and slice it finely, then separate into rings. Cut the ham into small strips, and the Danish Blue into small cubes. Layer all these ingredients or jumble them lightly in a glass bowl. Put the seasonings in a glass jar with a secure stopper. Add the oil and shake well to blend, then add the vinegar and shake to mix. Shake again and toss lightly with the salad just before serving.

Serves 4.

Trader Vic's Salad

Hawaii   Illustration page 71

INGREDIENTS	Imperial	Metric	American
Frozen peas	8 oz.	225 g.	1 1/4 cups
Frozen sweetcorn	8 oz.	225 g.	1 1/4 cups
Salt			
Can of pineapple pieces, drained	8 oz.	227 g.	8 oz.
Small sweet red pepper, de-seeded and chopped	1	1	1
Mayonnaise	3 tbsp.	3 tbsp.	3 tbsp.
Single (light) cream	2 tbsp.	2 tbsp.	2 tbsp.
Rind and juice of 1 small lemon			
Paprika			

Blanch the peas and sweetcorn in boiling salted water for 2 minutes. Drain and rinse under a cold tap. Mix the peas and sweetcorn with the pineapple pieces and pepper. Blend the mayonnaise with the cream, lemon rind and juice, and paprika. Toss with the vegetables and chill before serving.

Serves 4–6 as a side salad.

Domates Salata

Greece

INGREDIENTS	Imperial	Metric	American
New potatoes, boiled and diced	12 oz.	340 g.	2 cups
Medium-sized tomatoes skinned, de-seeded and chopped	8 oz.	225 g.	1 cup
Onion, finely chopped	1	1	1
Black olives, stoned	2 oz.	50 g.	1/4 cup
Mayonnaise	3 tbsp.	3 tbsp.	3 tbsp.
Milk	2 tbsp.	2 tbsp.	2 tbsp.
Black pepper			

Toss all the vegetables together. Mix the mayonnaise with the milk and pepper, and toss lightly with the vegetables, coating them evenly. Chill. Serves 4 as a side salad.

Calcutta Club Salad

India

INGREDIENTS	Imperial	Metric	American
Long grain rice	4 oz.	100 g.	7 tbsp.
Salt			
Frozen green beans	4 oz.	100 g.	1 cup
Button mushrooms, sliced	2 oz.	50 g.	2/3 cup
2 in/5 cm piece cucumber			
Curry paste	1–2 tsp.	1–2 tsp.	1–2 tsp.
Mayonnaise	3 tbsp.	3 tbsp.	3 tbsp.

Cook the rice in boiling salted water until tender. Drain and rinse under cold water. Cool. Blanch the beans in boiling salted water. Drain and rinse under cold water, and cool. Mix the rice, beans, mushrooms and cucumber in a bowl. Blend the curry paste into the mayonnaise and toss with the salad. Chill before serving.

Serves 4 as a side salad.

Domates Salata (*top*), Calcutta Club Salad (*centre*) and Trader Vic's Salad (*bottom*)

Two-Way Yoghurt Dressing

Greece and Turkey

INGREDIENTS	Imperial	Metric	American
First dressing			
Natural yoghurt	4 fl. oz.	100 ml.	1/2 cup
Soured cream	2 tbsp.	2 tbsp.	2 tbsp.
Mixed English mustard	1/4 tsp.	1/4 tsp.	1/4 tsp.
Lemon juice	1 tbsp.	1 tbsp.	1 tbsp.
Salt and pepper			
Second dressing			
Natural yoghurt	3 fl. oz.	75 ml.	1/3 cup
Whipping or single cream	4 tbsp.	4 tbsp.	4 tbsp.
Dijon mustard	1 tbsp.	1 tbsp.	1 tbsp.
Salt and pepper if needed			

Stir the yoghurt until smooth. Stir in the remaining ingredients for the dressing you choose. Taste and adjust the seasoning if needed. Cover and chill until needed. The dressing should thicken but not be solid. Makes 1/4 pt./ 150 ml./2/3 cup dressing.

You could make the second dressing with mayonnaise instead of yoghurt and add 2 tsp. lemon juice for extra tang. This version is called Creamy Mustard Mayonnaise.

Blue Cheese Dressing

U.S.A.

INGREDIENTS	Imperial	Metric	American
Blue cheese (Roquefort, Danish Blue, etc.)	2 oz.	50 g.	1/4 cup
Natural yoghurt	4 fl. oz.	100 ml.	1/2 cup
Strained lemon juice	1 tsp.	1 tsp.	1 tsp.
A few drops of clear honey (optional)			

Crumble the cheese finely. Put all the ingredients in a food processor and blend until smooth. Use cold over hot vegetables such as cauliflower or beetroot, or over a root vegetable salad or slaw.

Makes 6 fl. oz./175 ml./3/4 cup dressing.

Pitta Bread

Greece, Cyprus   Illustration page 33

INGREDIENTS	Imperial	Metric	American
Honey	1/2 tsp.	1/2 tsp.	1/2 tsp.
Warm water	1/2 pt.	300 ml.	1 1/4 cups
Fresh yeast	1 oz.	25 g.	1 oz.
Salt	2 tsp.	2 tsp.	2 tsp.
Bread flour	1 lb.	450 g.	1 lb.
Olive oil	2 tbsp.	2 tbsp.	2 tbsp.
Extra oil for brushing			

Dissolve the honey in half the water. Blend in the yeast. Leave until frothy. Mix the salt and flour in a bowl. Make a well in the centre, and pour in the yeast mixture. Add the oil and the remaining water, and pour into the bowl. Mix all the ingredients in the bowl to make a soft dough. Knead for a full 8 minutes, working the dough with your hands, or use a dough hook on a big electric mixer for 6 minutes. Shape the dough into an oval. Rub it with oil, and leave it in a warm place, covered with a cloth, for about 1 hour, until doubled in bulk. Punch it down and knead out any creases. Divide it into 4 equal-sized pieces. Roll into balls and leave to rise, uncovered, for 30 minutes.

Now roll the balls into flat ovals about 1/8 in/3 mm thick. Lay them on greased and floured baking sheets. Leave for another 30 minutes. Heat the oven to 475°F/ 240°C/Gas Mark 9. Bake the pitta for 10–12 minutes. Wrap in a cloth at once to soften the pitta and cool on a wire rack. Reheat gently in foil if you wish, at the edge of the barbecue.

Burger Buns or Hot Dog Rolls

International

INGREDIENTS	Imperial	Metric	American
Milk	4 fl. oz.	100 ml.	1/2 cup
Water	4 fl. oz.	100 ml.	1/2 cup
Clear honey	1½ tsp.	1½ tsp.	1½ tsp.
Dried yeast	1½ tsp.	1½ tsp.	1½ tsp.
Flour, white or 81% extraction (strong flour if possible)	12 oz.	340 g.	3 cups
Salt	1 tsp.	1 tsp.	1 tsp.

Mix the milk and water in a saucepan. Bring to hand-hot. Stir in the honey. Sprinkle the yeast on top. Leave in a fairly warm place for 10 minutes or until frothy. Sift the flour and salt into a bowl. Pour in the yeast liquid. Mix with a wooden spoon, then by hand until it coheres. (It may be sticky.) Turn out onto a well-floured board and knead until smooth. Put the dough back in the bowl and cover loosely with greased polythene. Leave in a warm place for 45 minutes–1 hour or until the dough has doubled its bulk.

Punch the dough down, knead it briefly, and divide it into 12 equal portions. Roll each into a ball. Flatten to about ¾ in/2 cm thick with your palm. Place well apart on a greased baking sheet. Leave in a warm place for about 40 minutes until puffy. Meanwhile heat the oven to 400°F/ 200°C/Gas Mark 6.

Bake the buns for 15–20 minutes. Wrap them in a cloth at once and cool on a wire rack.

For Hot Dog Rolls shape the dough into 8 cylinders or rolls instead of balls. Do not flatten them. Prove and bake them like round buns. Cool in a cloth on a wire rack.

DESSERTS

A bowl of mixed fresh fruit, especially fresh apricots, peaches and citrus fruits is all that people in hot countries generally offer as a barbecue dessert, and it's usually enough. Americans and Europeans tend to like a cake, flan, sweet fondue, or even a gâteau which has to be eaten with a spoon.

Dutch Fried Apple Cake

Holland

INGREDIENTS	Imperial	Metric	American
For the base			
Unsalted butter	4 oz.	100 g.	½ cup
Digestive biscuits, crushed	6 oz.	175 g.	1 cup
Large apples, peeled and sliced	2	2	2
Sultanas (golden raisins)	4 oz.	100 g.	1 cup

	Imperial	Metric	American
For the filling			
Gouda cheese, finely grated	9 oz.	250 g.	2 cups
Flour	3 tbsp.	3 tbsp.	3 tbsp.
Single (light) cream	4½ tbsp.	4½ tbsp.	4½ tbsp.
Mixed spice	½ tsp.	½ tsp.	½ tsp.
Grated rind and juice of 1 lemon			
Eggs, separated	3	3	3
Caster sugar	4 oz.	100 g.	½ cup
For decoration			
Red-skinned apples, cored and sliced	2	2	2
Apricot jam sieved	2 tbsp.	2 tbsp.	2 tbsp.

Melt half the butter in a saucepan, and stir in the biscuit crumbs. Press the mixture into the base of a loose-bottomed 8 in/20 cm cake tin.

Fry the apple slices in the remaining butter until just soft and golden. Drain off any free fat. Cool the apples slightly, then spread over the biscuit crumb base. Scatter the sultanas on top. Heat the oven to 350°F/180°C/Gas Mark 4.

Mix together the grated cheese, flour, cream, mixed spice and the grated rind and juice of the lemon. Mix the egg yolks and sugar together, and stir into the cheese mixture, blending evenly. Whisk the egg whites until stiff but not dry and fold them in. Turn the cheese mixture gently into the tin. Bake for 45–50 minutes. Cool in the tin on a wire rack.

When cold, arrange the apple slices for decoration in rings around the top of the cake. Warm the apricot jam until liquid, and brush it over them.

Serves 8–10.

Half-way between a cake and a cheesecake, this cake is firm enough to be eaten without a spoon, yet can equally well be served as a dessert with cream. It makes a super alternative to a classic apple pie and is much easier to manage. It also keeps excellently.

Gingerbread

International

INGREDIENTS	Imperial	Metric	American
Flour	1 lb.	450 g.	4 cups
Ground ginger	3 tsp.	3 tsp.	3 tsp.
Baking powder	3 tsp.	3 tsp.	3 tsp.
Bicarbonate of soda (baking soda)	1 tsp.	1 tsp.	1 tsp.
Salt	1 tsp.	1 tsp.	1 tsp.
Demerara sugar	8 oz.	225 g.	1 cup
Unsalted butter	6 oz.	175 g.	¾ cup
Black treacle (molasses)	6 oz.	175 g.	½ cup
Golden syrup (light molasses)	6 oz.	175 g.	½ cup
Egg, beaten	1	1	1
Milk	½ pt.	300 ml.	1¼ cups

Grease and line a deep 9 in/22.5 cm square cake tin. Sift together all the dry ingredients except the sugar into a large bowl. Put the sugar, butter, treacle and syrup in a saucepan and warm until the butter has just melted. Mix the egg into the milk. Stir the melted mixture into the middle of the dry ingredients, then mix in the milk. Beat thoroughly with a wooden spoon. Pour the mixture into the prepared tin and bake at 350°F/180°C/Gas Mark 4 for 1½ hours or until the gingerbread is springy in the centre. Leave to cool in the tin, then turn out onto a wire rack to cool. When cold, wrap in foil without removing the lining paper and store for 4–6 days before cutting into squares.

Gingerbread is one of the best finger-food desserts to serve at a barbecue. Its spicy flavour complements the grilled food perfectly. It is excellent with fruit or cheese, or just buttered; or if you like you can serve it with dollops of whipped cream. As a bonus, you can make it almost a week ahead.

Gingerbread with Scandinavian Pea Soup, page 31

Walnut and Fruit Roll

France

INGREDIENTS	Imperial	Metric	American
Margarine and flour for baking tin			
Large eggs	*4*	*4*	*4*
Caster sugar	*3 oz.*	*75 g.*	*3/8 cup*
Walnut pieces, ground	*1 1/2 oz.*	*40 g.*	*1 1/2 oz.*
Flour	*1 1/2 oz.*	*40 g.*	*1/3 cup*
Pinch of cinnamon			
Stork margarine, melted	*1 oz.*	*25 g.*	*2 tbsp.*
Icing sugar			
For the filling			
Double cream	*1/2 pt.*	*300 ml.*	*1 1/4 cups*
Caster sugar to taste			
Raspberries or other soft fruit, e.g. sliced strawberries	*12 oz.*	*340 g.*	*1 1/2 cups*
For decoration			
Double cream (or UHT aerosol cream as needed)	*1/4 pt.*	*150 ml.*	*2/3 cup*

Line a 14 × 10 in/35 cm × 25 cm Swiss roll tin with greaseproof paper, greased and floured. Heat the oven to 375°F/190°C/Gas Mark 5. Whisk together the eggs and sugar until very thick and creamy. Fold in the walnuts with a metal spoon, then sift and fold in the flour and cinnamon. Fold in the melted margarine. Spread evenly in the tin. Bake for 15–20 minutes until the sponge is springy. Loosen from the edges of the tin with a knife point, and turn out onto a large sheet of greaseproof paper dusted with sifted icing sugar. Peel off the lining paper. Leave to cool.

Trim off the edges of the sponge. Whip the cream for the filling stiffly, sweetening with a little caster sugar. Spread the cream over the sponge. Reserve a few raspberries for decoration and spread the rest over the cream to within 1/2 in/1 cm of the edge of the sponge. Fold over one long side gently by lifting the greaseproof paper; the edge of the sponge should overlap the other edge slightly. Tuck the overlap underneath with the flat side of a knife blade. Then tip the roll onto a sheet of foil with the cut edges underneath. Fold up the foil to enclose the roll. Chill for 30 minutes.

To serve, bring the roll to room temperature. Whip the cream for decoration lightly. Unwrap the roll and tip it onto a serving dish. Spread it thinly with whipped cream, pipe cream rosettes down the centre top, and decorate with the reserved raspberries.

The part of France called Perigord is famous for its walnuts and orchard fruit. When soft fruit is out of season, you could fill the roll with 6–8 fl. oz./175–225 ml. stiff apple purée mixed with 2 oz./50 g. sultanas and a little lemon juice and use fresh or canned stoned cherries.

DRINKS

Keep drinks simple – and plentiful. Use big mugs rather than cups, and plastic glasses for soft drinks because people tend to leave them around on the ground. As a beverage, most people now prefer coffee to tea. As for other drinks, beer is always popular with men, certainly at an informal barbecue, although a simple choice of red and white wine always makes summer drinking a pleasure. Keep it chilled 'on site' in a bucket or tin bath of broken or dry ice.

If you have a barman to serve it, your guests will enjoy a cold fruit punch, or, for a cold-weather barbecue mulled ale or cider.

Always serve at least one long soft drink such as Spiced Tomato Juice, and have plenty of fruit juices for children.

Port-of-Call Party Punch

International   Illustration on cover

INGREDIENTS	Imperial	Metric	American
Burgundy wine	1 qrt.	1.1 l.	5 cups
Port wine	4 fl. oz.	100 ml.	½ cup
Cherry brandy	2 fl. oz.	50 ml.	¼ cup
Juice of 1½ lemons			
Juice of 3 oranges			
Caster sugar	2 oz.	50 g.	¼ cup
Soda water	1 qrt.	1.1 l.	5 cups
Fresh fruit			

Mix all the ingredients except the sugar and soda water. Add most or all of the sugar to suit your taste; stir it until it dissolves. Pour the mixture over a large block of ice in a punch bowl. Just before serving, add the soda water.
Serves 6–8.

Spiced Tomato Juice

U.S.A.

INGREDIENTS	Imperial	Metric	American
Whole cloves	4	4	4
Celery tops with leaves	3	3	3
Tomato juice	1¼ pts.	750 ml.	3 cups
Water	8 fl. oz.	225 ml.	1 cup
Golden granulated sugar	1 tbsp.	1 tbsp.	1 tbsp.
Worcestershire sauce	1 tsp.	1 tsp.	1 tsp.
Pinch of cayenne pepper			
Salt	¼ tsp.	¼ tsp.	¼ tsp.
Lemon juice	2 tsp.	2 tsp.	2 tsp.

Tie the cloves and celery tops in a piece of cloth. Put all the ingredients in a saucepan and simmer for 20 minutes uncovered. Strain into a jug, cool and chill. Can be stored in the refrigerator in a jar with a well-fitting lid for 3–4 days.

Mulled Cider

England

INGREDIENTS	Imperial	Metric	American
Medium dry cider (alcoholic)	1 qrt.	1.1 l.	2½ pts.
Muscovado sugar	1½ oz.	40 g.	8 tsp.
Pinch of salt			
Whole cloves	4	4	4
Piece of cinnamon stick 2 in/5 cm long			
Allspice berries	4	4	4
Strip of orange peel			

Put the cider, sugar and salt in a saucepan. Tie the spices loosely in a piece of cloth and add it. Bring gently to the boil, cover and simmer for 12–15 minutes. Serve hot in mugs.
Serves 4.

CLEARING UP

Douse your fire as soon as cooking is finished (page 19). Foil parcels which hold the heat well, will cope with the needs of any stray searcher after food. They can be left on the side of the barbecue until it cools down enough to be handled.

If possible, put the tools and racks into a 'soak' of very hot water laced with strong detergent while still hot. A tin bath or empty beer barrel is ideal for this, filled with a hose from your kitchen tap. Keep the container out of the kitchen, however, until the rest of your clearing-up is done. Ideally, leave it alone overnight.

As soon as the barbecue can be handled, deal with the fuel and fire-pan. Transfer the coals to a bucket if you have not already done so, so that the unused fuel and ash for garden use can be separated later. If you have a layer of gravel in the bottom of your fire-pan, it may be greasy, so shovel it into a separate bucket with hot water and detergent to soak. Dry it thoroughly before re-use.

If you have lined your fire-pan with foil, it should only need rubbing with a wire brush or wire wool, and dusting off. If it is very dirty, try oven-cleaner while it is still warm and scour it, then rinse with hot water. (Wear rubber gloves for this.)

If this seems too much to do after a late-night party, brush out any solid bits of burned food with a stiff brush, then use the oven-cleaner technique or a special barbecue cleaner in the morning. Rinse, scour and re-rinse racks and tools then too.

Don't attempt to do much general clearing up after a late-night party. In the dark, when one is tired, it's all too easy to crush underfoot a stray glass left on the ground, and you're certain to miss knives and forks left around. If you've put out clearly-marked rubbish bags (page 16) you should, with luck, not face too much general litter next day.

Put on your favourite cassettes or radio programme to help you through aftermath chores. (There may be some punch left, if you're lucky!)

One last task! It's wise to put a thin film of oil on racks, skewers and tools as soon as they are well dried, even if you are only putting them away for a short time. Damp-weather rust can attack them quickly. If you are putting them away for the winter, this step is vital – although once you've got barbecuing 'buttoned up', you'll almost certainly want to do it year-round.

INDEX

Figures in italics refer to illustrations.